.rvice

. .~~4 о61511

Poking seaweed with a stick
and running away from the smell

ABERDEENSHIRE
LIBRARIES

DRAWN
LIBRARY

D0414901

Poking seaweed with a stick
and running away from the smell

ALISON WHITELOCK

First published in 2008 by Wakefield Press, Australia
First UK edition published in 2009 by Polygon,
an imprint of Birlinn Ltd

West Newington House
10 Newington Road
Edinburgh
EH9 1QS

www.birlinn.co.uk
9 8 7 6 5 4 3 2 1

FT Pbk

Copyright © Alison Whitelock, 2008

All rights reserved. No part of this publication may
be reproduced, stored, or transmitted in any form, or
by any means electronic, mechanical or photocopying,
recording or otherwise, without the express written
permission of the publisher.

The right of Alison Whitelock to be identified as the author
of this work has been asserted in accordance with
the Copyright, Designs and Patents Act 1988.

ISBN 978 1 84697 045 0

British Library Cataloguing-in-Publication Data
A catalogue record for this book is available
on request from the British Library.

Typeset in Goudy Old Style at Birlinn

Printed and bound in Great Britain
by CPI Antony Rowe, Chippenham, Wiltshire

For Mum

Contents

Retard dad

My brother Andrew's written a song and he's putting a
band together. He just calls himself 'Andy' and musicians
are queuing up to play with him. Andrew's been really
angry for a long time and great things can come out
of talent and pain. This song he just wrote, he says it's
amazing, says he plays it every single day and even *he's*
not fed up with it yet. He calls it 'Retard Dad' and says
he'll be playing it at the Glastonbury Festival next year on
the newcomers' stage. Andrew's first gig at Glastonbury,
I wouldn't miss it for the world. I'm so proud of him and
if you knew what Andrew had been through, you'd be
proud of him too.

My da was a crazy man, see, and he made our lives
miserable. He killed a puppy once when we were young
– kicked it to death right there in front of us. He resented
every animal that we ever brought home and we were
animal daft, always bringing home cats and dogs and

ducks and donkeys and anything we found in the street that looked like it might be in need of a good home and often others that weren't in need of a good home at all.

Lots of bad stuff happened in our lives, but one of the best things that ever happened was that finally, at the age of 59, after 40 years of abuse, Mum found the courage to say 'No more'. She threw a few bits into her tartan holdall, put the dogs and the cats into the back of the car and finally she left him. And I've never been more proud.

After she was gone I thought about him and through the cracks in the doors of my mind I could see him there at home by himself, with nobody. He's wishing he'd been a better father, that he'd been there for us, that he could remember our birthdays for Chrissake. And next thing I know my eyes are welling up and a lump's appearing in my throat and I start thinking about how things could have been and what a waste of time that is.

Mum, though, she's making up for wasted time. She's bought herself a wee flat and a fancy wee car, and she's started placing discreet ads in the lonely-hearts columns in the local paper. She's decorated her new pad on a jungle theme, so African masks and elephant trunks adorn the walls. Her life-size sculpture of a Zulu warrior holding a spear – she carted it back from the south of France wrapped in a sleeping bag – stands in the corner and doubles as a hat stand, and two bongo drums sit at each side of her king-size bed and double as bedside tables. She's finally getting to express herself and she's doing it in style – in fabrics and furs, in sculptures and in masks – and she doesn't care what anybody thinks. This is freedom and Mum likes the taste.

And every so often, in her wee dark moments, she thinks about how life might have been if she hadn't met him and she'd taken that interior design course instead. And she thinks about all the years she's wasted and what she *should* have done and what she *could* have done before she met him and got saddled with three kids, four dogs, five cats and a donkey called Annie.

She's coming down from Scotland for another visit to Sydney soon. She comes down twice a year to see us and last time she brought a fifteen-foot blow-up Santa Claus you plug in and it lights up the garden.

Some people might be embarrassed by what their mums do, but me, I couldn't be prouder. She's the best thing that ever happened in my life and I wouldn't change her and her fifteen-foot blow-up Santa Claus for all the bongos in the world.

Arsehole on a tandem

She was wearing her Audrey Hepburn hat and gloves to
match and a pair of winkle-pickers that would take your eye
out soon as look at you. And she'd bought herself some
stockings too, with a line up the back, and she turned the
head of every boy she passed in the street.

After mass that Sunday she stopped in at Angie's
sweetie shop for a stick of Wrigleys to chew on the long
walk home. When she came out of the shop she couldn't
help but notice the strange man sitting on the tandem
at the side of the road, by himself if you don't mind. She
unwrapped her stick of Wrigleys pretending she didn't
notice a thing and she'd no sooner set off on her long walk
home when the strange man was cycling up alongside her.
'Arsehole on a tandem,' she thought, as she tried to hide
her confusion at seeing a man riding a tandem on his own.
Then the man who would one day be my da jumped off his
tandem and stood sweating before the woman who would

one day be my mum and Mum said to him, 'Well, it's no' often you see a man riding a tandem by himself.' And the man who would one day be my da blurted out he'd seen her standing behind him in the queue at Angie's sweetie shop and that he'd fallen in love with her right there and then, and without taking a breath he asked Mum if she would go out on a date with him the following Saturday night. Mum, well, she didn't know where to look, and so she said yes but if he didn't mind, could he leave his tandem at home.

My da was the happiest man alive when he got back on his tandem and that's when he decided he was going to marry Mum and that he would ask her that Saturday night right after their date, if it was the last word he spoke.

The Saturday night came and my da was already waiting outside The Roxy when Mum arrived at six o'clock. He'd Brylcreemed his hair for her and put on some Old Spice and Mum felt sorry for him when she saw he'd cut himself shaving and left the toilet paper stuck to the wound. They hooked arms and walked up the steps to The Roxy looking just like a proper couple out on a date on a Saturday night and my da made a fuss of Mum that first night all right, buying the tickets and the choc-ices and everything. When the movie was over he wanted to escort Mum back home all safe and sound, but she wouldn't hear of it 'cause the bus that would take him all the way home was just across the road from The Roxy. So they walked together to the bus stop where she waited with him in the cold, and as they waited a thick fog descended upon them and the street lamps gave off an eerie yellow haze, much like the haze they'd seen just moments before in *Psycho* when Anthony Perkins goes up to the scary-looking house to see what the hell's wrong with his mother.

Mum was beautiful in this light, as he knew she would be in every light he saw her in thereafter, and he knew he was lucky she'd agreed to go on a date with him. He also knew if he didn't ask her to marry him that night, it was only a matter of time until she discovered that he was a complete prick and dumped him forever. He was dying for a fag but he'd wait until after he'd asked her to be his bride so his breath would be fresh in case she decided to kiss him passionately in the excitement of their future together. But the man who would one day be my da was scared. Scared she'd say no, that she'd laugh in his face and say something like, Me, marry you? You're fuckin' joking aren't you? Scared the number 64 bus would come when he'd only half the question out, scared he'd be ridiculed and left cycling on his tandem without a wife until the end of time.

His heart was thumping hard now and my da felt dizzy and intoxicated by the love he felt for Mum. His excitement mounted and suddenly he felt unstoppable. His desire to have her as his bride knew no bounds and in the heat of the moment, my da took Mum in his arms, lifted her off the ground and swung her lovingly around in a circle, and all the while his eyes never left hers, just like in the American movies they sometimes showed at The Roxy on a Saturday afternoon. My da turned Mum full circle and he'd no sooner placed her gently back onto her own two feet when something terrible happened, something he wished he could have prevented more than anything, something their children and their children's children would write about in years to come. It was at this – what should have been – most romantic of moments, that my da unfortunately farted. Not a silent unassuming kind of fart, but more a fog-horn kind of fart and, sure, it was foggy, but that one solitary, seemingly innocent fart ruined everything. He clenched his buttocks, albeit too late, but he clenched them nonetheless and he stared at her, his eyes wide in disbelief. And she stared back, her eyes wide in a similar kind of disbelief. And nobody said a word.

After an eternity, they heard the drone of the 64 bus as it made its way through the yellow fog. The bus stopped and its doors flew open and my da raced onto the bus, leaving Mum behind in the eerie yellow haze. He headed straight to the back of the bus, took out his packet of Woodbines and slumped down on the red vinyl seat. With his right cheek pressed against the window, he drew long and hard on his cigarette and stared out into the fog and he wished he could have disappeared into it. The cool windowpane did little to soothe his troubled mind.

A real pea souper

Of course she ended up marrying him and how could she have said no? She felt so sorry for him with the toilet paper stuck to his face and then the fart when all along he'd intended to propose. Really, she should have seen the signs right there and then, that the future she was about to sign up for was not exactly what she was hoping for. But Mum never reads the signs, 'cause she prefers to believe what she wants to believe, rather than accept what's obvious and staring her right in the face.

Mum looked beautiful on her wedding day when Grampa gave her away, and he wore a yellow rose in his buttonhole that he'd pinched from the rose bush that grew just behind his greenhouse. Nanny made a garland for Mum's hair from Grampa's pink and white rose bushes and when she placed it on Mum's head, her long blonde locks nestled themselves between the buds and her pale-green eyes came alive. Her wedding dress was made of white lace (and, my, how it burned that day years later when she set fire to it), and the jewels around her neck sparkled in what little spring sunlight there was on offer that Friday the thirteenth of May. When the organist played the first few notes of 'Here Comes the Bride' she walked inside, arm in arm with Grampa, and her smile lit up the chapel and Grampa was more than a little sad to be giving away one so beautiful to one who wasn't unlike Anthony Perkins himself.

It was two years after they'd seen *Psycho* that my sister Izzy was born at Beckford Lodge Hospital in Hamilton, twelve miles from Glasgow, in a nice white sterile environment with all the best of medical care. And two years after Izzy was born, it was me who appeared, and another two years after that, it was Andrew.

I was expected on 9 November 1964. Once Mum's contractions started, she yelled out for my da to get the doctor and so he jumped from the couch and grabbed the keys for the single-decker bus he'd got cheap from Hamish at the bus depot, pulled on his donkey jacket and ran as fast as he could out into the night. Nine months had passed already and he knew she was going to have to drop it soon, what with her barely able to unload the lorry these past few weeks when the coal got delivered.

Mum's mum had a feeling it would all happen that night so she took the number 73 bus to the Dalton Road end and walked the four miles to our cottage at Back-O-Hill, out there in the middle of nowhere, and far away from a nice white sterile environment and all the best of medical care. Back-O-Hill means 'back of the hill', but there wasn't any hill, just fields and windy roads and our stone cottage right there in the middle of the green.

'It was a real pea souper that night,' Mum said. 'Couldnae see two feet in front of you.' It was much talked about, the fog that year; they still talk about it today. They called it the worst pea souper of 1964 and I think they may even have written a song about it, I mean it was a *big* event at the time.

My da raced into the thick darkness and tried to remember where he'd parked the bus and he swallowed the fog like lumps of cotton wool as he groped for the door handle, and when he found it he nearly pulled it off its hinges as he yanked it open and jumped in. 'Start for fuckssake, will ye!' he growled as he pumped the accelerator. It started, thank Christ, and he turned on the headlights, though he may as well have not bothered for all the light they gave off. Straight ahead, he drove, with his nose stuck against the frozen windscreen, peering through a spot where the heat of his own breath had melted the ice, then onto the windy road and four miles to town where Doctor McNamara was tucked up in bed sound asleep, delivering babies the last thing on her mind.

He was no sooner off into the fog than Mum's contractions got really serious and, quick as a flash, Nanny was boiling pots of water and gathering up linen from all corners of the house. The telly was blaring in the corner and *Coronation Street* came on and Mum watched it to try and keep her mind off giving birth to me. *In* and *out*, she focused on her breathing, *in* and *out*, just like Doctor McNamara had told her.

The first half of *Coronation Street* came and went and Mum, still trying to keep her mind off the pain, started singing out loud with the adverts as they came on.

> *Abercrombie biscuits are the best,*
> *In your tummy, they digest,*
> *In the bathroom they go west,*
> *Abercrombie biscuits are the best,*
> *Try some – tomorrow!*

Mum was in a world of her own making up her own lyrics and Nanny looked on thinking pain can sometimes make people behave in strange ways.

The second half of *Coronation Street* was about to start and Doctor McNamara still hadn't made an appearance. Mum called out to me in that dark belly of hers, 'Please just wait, will ye! Just calm yourself wee yin!' But unfortunately I couldn't wait and suddenly my head started to appear. There was a lot of pushing and shoving going on, with

Nanny there waiting for me yelling out instructions that Mum didn't dare disobey – until with one final almighty push, the perfect delivery took place right there in the kitchen of our cottage at Back-O-Hill.

Nanny cut the cord and held me in her arms while Mum lay there on her back, worn out and glad it was all over. When Nanny handed me to her wrapped in a shawl, Mum held me close to her chest and whispered in my ear that I was an impatient wee fucker and could I no' have waited for Doctor McNamara to arrive. I'm still impatient today and you know how families are, they don't let you forget anything.

Then suddenly, from the pea soup, Mum and Nanny could hear the *clip clop, clip clop* of two coconut shells being banged together. As the sound got closer they realised it was Doctor McNamara's horse's hooves outside on the wee footpath leading up to the front door of the cottage, accompanied by the slow murmur of the engine of the single-decker bus as my da and Doctor McNamara arrived on the scene together, albeit too late, for my arrival. They raced inside only to discover mother, grandmother and baby were all doing just fine without anybody's help, thank you very much, and Doctor McNamara was none too chuffed, as you can imagine, at being prised from her bed on such a pea souper only to arrive on the scene to find the job done by the grandmother of all people. And so the silly big cow took the huff and turned on her heels and fumbled her way back through the fog, mounted her steed and fucked off in a right temper.

My da, exhausted by the whole proceedings, lay down on the couch and fell asleep as Mum and Nanny looked at each other and wondered what men were made of these days. He fell asleep with his mouth wide open and Mum was tempted to feed him the afterbirth, but decided it was too good for him and asked Nanny to fry it up and feed it to the dogs instead.

The next morning, I woke Mum early and she filled an empty two-litre Treetop Orange bottle with milk and stuck a teat on the end of it and I sucked away on that until I fell asleep right there in her arms. She held me close to her heart and stepped outside where the soothing wind blew through her long golden hair and it felt good.

And now she had another wee life to care for, as if she didn't have problems enough, what with him and his drinking and his womanising.

The fog, now more a consommé, had lifted a good deal and Mum could make out the barn and the dry-stane dyke at the far end of the green land. The clean fresh air felt cool in her lungs and as she looked down, she noticed that Doctor McNamara's horse had left a big pile of shite on the path just outside the front door.

'Shitey luck's good luck,' Mum said out loud, as she stared into the horizon and rocked me gently in her arms.

My best pal

We moved quite soon after I was born, away from Back-O-Hill in the middle of nowhere to the same town Mum used to live in when she met my da. The school I went to was just a short walk away from our house and that was brilliant, 'cause it meant I could go home and see Mum every day at lunchtime. I was scared to go to school on that first day 'cause I didn't have any pals, but when I got there I met Maggie, and me and Maggie became best pals on that first day and spent the whole of that day together, playing with the big bucket of crayons the teacher gave us. Maggie's favourite crayons were the blue ones, and my favourites were the blue ones too. When the bell rang for playtime, me and Maggie went outside and played on the climbing frame and Maggie hung from it, pretending to be a monkey. But she looked nothing like a monkey, she had long, shiny chestnut hair all the way to her waist and pink rosy cheeks, and everybody knew, just by looking at her, that one day she'd be famous and I thought that maybe if I was her pal, some day I'd be famous too.

We sat beside each other every day after that and then we even started going to each other's houses at lunchtime. Sometimes when we went to my house, Mum would make us a fried sausage each and one day when we went to Maggie's house, her Mum made us macaroni and cheese out of a tin and it was pure brilliant.

Me and Maggie loved to sing together and sometimes we made up our own songs and other times we sang the classics. My favourite was 'You are my Sunshine', but Maggie liked 'Nothing could be finer than to be in Carolina in the Morning'. And one day the singing teacher at school said we were the best singers in the class if not the entire school and when she said that, me and Maggie decided we were going to be professional singers on a proper stage one day. Then we started to dream about stardom, like Shirley Temple and Lena Zavaroni had. Lena Zavaroni was Scotland's answer to Shirley Temple and she shot to stardom when she was ten and by the time she was 35 she'd starved herself to death, 'cause the fame was all too much for her.

One day our headmistress, Miss Fairly, came to our class. When she walked in we all stood up and said, 'Good morning, Miss Fairly,' all at the same time and then she said, 'Good morning, class. Be seated.'

Miss Fairly had come to tell us she'd heard what great singers me and Maggie were and then she said she wouldn't be surprised if we went on to become the next Lena Zavaronis and I didn't know where to look. Then she said she wanted us to go around the school and sing a song to every class and so we did and all the classes loved us and after every song me and Maggie took a bow, 'cause that's what you do when you're on a real stage.

As we went from class to class, Maggie asked me what I'd do with all the money we were going to make once we went professional. I said I'd buy all the tinned macaroni and cheese that money could buy and Maggie said she'd do the same 'cause that's what best pals do.

Now that Maggie had said I was her best pal, she said I should sleep over at her house so we could practise our songs. So I went to Maggie's house the next Wednesday after school and we practised in Maggie's living room till *Coronation Street* came on and Maggie's da said he wanted peace and quiet to watch it. So Maggie took me upstairs to her bedroom to show me where I'd be sleeping that night and when she put the light on, I saw something more gorgeous than anything I'd ever seen in my entire life. Maggie's dressing table was painted gold with gold shiny knobs and fairy lights around the mirror and the stool was painted gold too and had a pink furry seat. And when Maggie sat down at her dressing table, she looked just like a princess with her long shiny chestnut hair and her pink rosy cheeks, and as I stood behind her, I caught sight of my reflection in the mirror and I looked like Maggie's ugly sister so I turned my head away quickly and looked out Maggie's bedroom window and down at her da's cabbage patch. Out of the corner of my eye I watched Maggie as she took out her lipstick from the pink purse she kept in the gold drawer. She ran the pink lipstick across her lips and then asked me if I wanted to put some on too and I said no, 'cause I didn't want to have to see myself up close in the mirror standing next to Maggie with her long chestnut hair and her pink rosy cheeks and now the painted lips.

And I wished I was beautiful like Maggie, but I wasn't. I was ugly, with my yellow hair that Mum had permed with the left-over perming lotion she had put under the sink after doing Auntie Annie's hair, and the more I thought about it, the more I started to wonder why Maggie would want to be pals with the likes of me. Then I got this sinking feeling right down deep inside my belly and knew right there and then that some day Maggie would leave me for another pal, a pal more beautiful than me and a pal who could sing better than me. And next thing you knew it would be Maggie and her new best pal owning all the tinned macaroni and cheese that money could buy.

The banana box in the attic

She wasn't out to buy anything in particular that day but the minute Mum walked into Big Marion's Second Hand Bargains on the Glasgow Road she saw it, way up on top of a dusty pile of second-hand fake oriental rugs that nearly reached the ceiling.

'Hey, Marion, is that a stuffed Airedale Terrier with wee wheels on its feet you've got up there, darlin'?' Mum asked.

Marion took the fag out of her mouth and nodded as the smoke rose up in front of her face, dyeing the front of her grey hair yellow.

'I think it is, Betty,' she said as she exhaled the smoke. 'Wait a sec and I'll get Jimmy in here wi' the ladder tout suite and you can get a look at it.'

'Only if you're sure it's nae bother, Marion. I fancy getting it for my lassie Ali's birthday, she'll be seven next week, but I don't want Jimmy going to any trouble if he's busy.'

'Och, it's nae bother, Betty. And don't worry about Jimmy, that useless bastard of mine's got to do something to earn his keep.'

Marion let out a huge yell: 'Oy, oor Jimmy! Get yersel' in here right now, by the way. I've a customer that wants a look at that Airedale wi' the wheels on its feet!'

'Right, I'm comin',' Jimmy yelled back from the office. 'I'll be there in a minute!' And a minute later Jimmy was on the scene and he smiled at Mum while he waited for instructions from big Marion.

'Get the ladder and get the Airedale down for Betty straightaway, Jimmy. She's thinking of getting it for her lassie Ali – it's her birthday next week.'

'Nae bother, Betty, I'll have it doon for you in a jiffy,' Jimmy said.

And so he leaned the ladder against the pile of oriental rugs and blankets and lost his footing once or twice as he climbed, then a few minutes later he was back down, proudly clutching the Airedale and beaming at Marion as if he'd just done something worthy of praise. Marion took the Airedale from him without so much as looking at him and put it on the counter.

'Aye, so there it is, Betty. Lovely coat it has on it, eh? Just like the real thing.'

'Aye, lovely right enough, Marion. And look at the

lovely wee wheels and the painted red handle for pushing it. Oor Ali'll love that. Animal daft so she is – always bringing home some bloody cat or dog that she finds in the street in need of a good home. Mind you, our Izzy's even worse. In fact, Ali brought a wee dog home just the other day, so she did, golden Labrador wi' four wee white feet. Lovely wee animal, you shoulda seen it. Soxy we called it, you know, looked like it was wearing four wee white socks. But och, the owner came and knocked on the door that night and claimed it back and Ali's distraught.'

'Poor wee mite, she must be heartbroken. This wee Airedale might be just the ticket to take her mind off him,' Marion said as she exhaled another lungful of yellow smoke.

'Och, aye, I mean she is heartbroken. But, mind you Marion, we've still a house full of fuckin' animals – you know, there's Toni and her litter of kittens, then Buster, Tich, Mitzie and Heidi the dogs – not to mention the ducks and Annie the fuckin' donkey.'

'Youse have a fair amount of animals right enough, Betty. Oh well, it's maybe as well you get her something that doesn't need any feeding, eh? This could be just the job.'

'Aye, I think you're right, Marion. How much do you want for it, hen?'

'Well, Betty, you're a good customer, so how about I do a special price for you darlin' – just a pound'll be fine.'

'Oh, that's lovely, Marion. Here's the pound and thanks. I'll take it wi' me now and gie it a wee shampoo before I go and get Ali from school. She'll be that delighted.'

'Okay, darlin', I'll get that useless bastard of mine to wrap it up for you – newspaper all right for you?'

'Aye, that's fine, Marion, thanks very much.'

'Nae bother, Betty. Any time.'

And so Jimmy wrapped up the Airedale Terrier on wheels and left the red painted handle sticking out and Mum took it home and shampooed it and left it out in the wind to dry and the next week when it was my birthday, I couldn't believe my eyes. I fell in love with my stuffed Airedale Terrier on wheels the minute I saw her and I took her outside onto the street and pushed her up and down and every so often I had to bend down to remove bits of gravel that got stuck in the solid rubber wheels. I called my stuffed Airedale Terrier Molly, and I took Molly everywhere with me. I was the envy of the street. At night I'd park her right next to my side of the bed and I'd lie there with my hand sticking out from under the blankets holding onto the red painted handle. Molly was mine and nobody else's but one night Andrew said that Molly was his, so I booted him on the shins and ran away and he ran after me and attacked me with the Hoover and of course it all ended in tears.

It was a hot day that day and I was sitting on the back step even though Mum said I'd get piles if I did. I didn't care. With the sun on my face I looked down at the tar on the path beneath my feet; the heat had softened it and I pressed my fingers into it and their imprints remained. Molly sat beside me at the side of the step and every now and again I stood up and pushed her up and down the soft tar, looking back to marvel at the wheel tracks and footprints we left behind. Then Mum told me to park Molly somewhere and to get inside and have my tea straightaway, but I told her I didn't want to leave Molly outside on the soft tar by herself and she told me to stop being stupid and if I didn't get inside and have my tea that minute, she'd put Molly in the loft and shut the lid and that would be the end of that. So I did as I was told and came inside and had my tea.

After my tea I was supposed to do the hoovering and the dishes but I couldn't wait to get back out to Molly and the sunshine and the soft tar. Just as I was about to put the last of my fried eggs on toast in my mouth, I heard my da pull his lorry into the driveway, then I heard the awful screeching of tyres and the mangling of metal. I dropped my fork and ran to the back door just in time to see one of Molly's wheels roll past the step where I'd get piles and out the gate and onto the street. Then I looked across at my da who was getting out of his lorry to see what the hell he had run over, and that's when I saw Molly crushed under the front wheel of my da's lorry, almost mangled beyond recognition.

I ran to the scene but there was nothing I could do. Molly was dead and my da was shouting and screaming and right bloody mad at me 'cause the red paint from Molly's handle had marked the silver bumper of his lorry and that's when he threatened to give me the hiding of my life.

I took off down the driveway after Molly's runaway wheel and when I caught it, I picked it up and cradled it in my cupped hands then ran to my room where I knew I'd be safe and far away from my da and his shouting. I wished I hadn't parked Molly outside with the sun shining and the tar melting, but I did, and now Molly was gone and my da was sayin' that's what you get when you're selfish and careless and don't look after toys that he pays good money for and is it any wonder he takes a drink and comes home in a right bloody temper.

My da was right. I hadn't taken good enough care of Molly and I felt ashamed and I cried. I kept Molly's wheel under my pillow for days and my da told me to stop snivelling and to grow up and then he told me I shouldn't be wasting my time playing with stupid dogs on wheels and soft tar when there was dishes and hoovering to be done. And then he said I was so careless I didn't deserve anything and I knew he was right, 'cause then I remembered the time I took Bluey our budgie out of his cage to clean it and when I wasn't looking Quackers, our one-eyed cat, sneaked up from behind and ate Bluey right there in front of me. Bluey put up a struggle, mind you, but it wasn't enough and once the struggle was over, his blue and yellow feathers were everywhere and I had to get the Hoover out before my da got home. My da said Bluey died because of my carelessness and now look, Molly was dead too.

With Molly dead and the memory of Bluey's blue and yellow feathers still fresh in my mind, I made a promise to myself right there and then there would be no more time for fun and track marks and fingerprints in soft tar and for pushing stupid stuffed animals on wheels with bright red handles up and down the street. From that moment on, I was going to be careful and responsible, and years later when my da was attacked by his business partner in an empty car park on the other side of town, it was me who'd be careful and responsible and drag his bleeding body to the car and race him to the hospital.

And so when I was seven I put all my toys away in a banana box, including Molly's wheel, and that was the last time I lost myself in play. Now I am older people ask me what it is I do for fun and I think back to the soft tar and Molly's wheel and I can't give them an answer because I don't know. I've forgotten how to play and how to have fun and I long for careless moments with Molly again.

Every so often I think about bringing my banana box out of the attic, and once I've done the hoovering and the dusting, that's precisely what I'll do.

The day Fiona got a brain tumour

Mrs Cameron was just about to start reading chapter two of *The Three Golliwogs* to us when Fiona burst in through the green painted doors and ran to Mrs Cameron, threw her arms around her neck and wouldn't let go. There were tears like I'd never seen before, and then uncontrollable wailing, and Mrs Cameron took Fiona out into the playground and closed the green painted doors behind her. My best pal Maggie ran up to the door and looked through the keyhole and the whole class held their breaths trying to hear what was wrong with Fiona, but all we could hear were her sobs.

Mrs Cameron came back inside and told us all to behave ourselves, that Fiona wasn't well and that she was going to take her to Miss Fairly, the headmistress, and that she'd be back directly. She told Maggie to read *The Three Golliwogs* to the class until she got back, then she shut the green painted doors behind her again and all of us rushed to the window to watch Mrs Cameron take Fiona across the playground and into the main school building to Miss Fairly's office. When Mrs Cameron came back, she told us Fiona's mammy was coming to take her home and that we should all try to settle down now and concentrate on *The Three Golliwogs*. I tried to do as Mrs Cameron told us but I was scared, 'cause it didn't seem right that somebody would burst in through the green painted doors like that if something terrible wasn't going on.

Then one morning before our milk break Mrs Cameron told us to behave ourselves, that she had something important to tell us and that important thing was that Fiona had a brain tumour. Timmy Strachan put his hand up and asked Mrs Cameron what a brain tumour was and so she told us. That's when all of us wished Timmy Strachan would just sit on his arse and mind his own business. And Mrs Cameron told us the doctor would have to operate on Fiona's head and that meant they would have to shave her hair off 'cause 'you can't have hair in the way when you're operating inside someone's head, now can you?'

Fiona didn't come to school for a long time after that. Then one day she did come and it was true, her head had been shaved and not only that but she walked slower than before. And when she looked at you her eyes seemed far away, and when she spoke her words came out slow.

When playtime came around that day all of us let Fiona stand by herself in the playground by the steps and she watched us all as we ran around and laughed together. As I ran with my best pal Maggie, I saw Fiona pull up the hood of her black duffle coat to keep her shaved head warm and I watched her as she pulled the coat tight around her body to keep the cold lonely air out.

Life went along like that for Fiona for another two weeks until one morning Fiona didn't come in through the green painted doors. That was the day Mrs Cameron told us to behave ourselves, that she had something important to tell us and that important thing was that, at only nine years old, Fiona was dead. She said that we should try not to be scared, sometimes terrible things like that just happened to people and nobody knew why and that's when Timmy Strachan put his hand up and asked Mrs Cameron why God let terrible things like that just happen to little girls at nine years old and again we all wished he would just sit on his arse and mind his own business. Then Mrs Cameron said we should take out *The Folk of the Faraway Tree* from our desks and she started to read where she'd left off the day before, but none of us had the mind for the folk of the faraway tree and their antics, what with Fiona being dead. And when we went into the playground at playtime that day none of us ran and none of us laughed and all of us stood by the steps and thought about Fiona. I thought about that day I saw her standing by herself in the very spot I was standing in now and I remembered her pulling up the hood of her black duffle coat to keep her shaved head warm and then pulling her coat tight around her body to keep the cold lonely air out. And that's when I pulled up my own hood and my own black duffle coat tight around my body and I hoped that I'd never catch a brain tumour and die like that too.

Let's all go to the Clyde

We used to get singing lessons at school and Miss Bright was our singing teacher. She looked like she was 95 years old and she wore aqua-blue eyeshadow and peachy-pink face powder and at three o'clock every Tuesday afternoon she would get out the tape recorder to play cassettes of recorded singing lessons called *Singing Together*. The singers on the tape would sing lines from songs then leave a gap and we had to learn the songs and fill in the gaps when the singers stopped singing.

Miss Bright had been trained in classical music and she said when she was younger she could sing in any number of languages you care to mention. She was always going on about how we should all be learning to speak another language, when all we wanted to do was fill in the gaps on the cassette and go home.

One Tuesday afternoon Miss Bright asked if anybody could name another language apart from English and that's when Martin Sedgeworth said he knew another language and that that language was *swearing* and Miss Bright took the chalk from her desk and turned to the board and wrote 'Swedish' in big writing. Everybody laughed and Miss Bright, well, she wanted to know what was so funny and none of us dared tell her that Martin Sedgeworth had said 'swearing' and not 'Swedish' and Martin Sedgeworth was the hero of the day. Me, I got butterflies in my stomach 'cause I knew that French was another language but I didn't dare say anything in case everybody laughed at me too, so I just stayed silent and Miss Bright put the cassette on again and we filled in the gaps and eventually the bell rang and we all went home.

The following Tuesday, Miss Bright gave us a song-writing competition for our homework and I got nervous wondering how I was ever going to write a song and what if you had to sing it out in front of the class if you won? The song had to be about the River Clyde, which flowed all the way from Greenock to Lanark and we had to have it done by the next Tuesday at three o'clock. I was in a right state but my pal, Maggie, she got her mum to write her a brilliant song about the Clyde being magical and winding, and in line two she said its name would live forever in the hearts of many. When I read that, I knew that my song was rubbish and that it would be Maggie's mum and not me who would win the competition.

The Monday before we had to hand in our homework I

read my song over and over again and I was embarrassed to put it in the same pile as Maggie's mum's, what with her big words and fancy suggestions, and my song went like this:

> Let's all go to the Clyde,
> Let's all go today,
> Let's all go to the Clyde,
> F-o-r a hol-i-day.

But homework's homework and if you don't put it on the teacher's desk when you're supposed to, then you can find yourself in a world of shite and so I put it there, on the pile with the others, including Maggie's mum's, then I sat back in my chair again and Miss Bright put the cassette on and we filled in the gaps until the bell rang and we all went home.

The next Tuesday Miss Bright said she had chosen a winner and I looked at Maggie and she looked at me and we both knew that hers would win. In the excitement a fight broke out between Timmy Strachan and Geraldine Cochrane who were fighting about whose song was the best and Miss Bright stepped in and said she'd never stand for anything like that in her classroom: if they didn't sit down and behave themselves then she wouldn't announce the winner for another week. So Timmy and Geraldine sat down and Miss Bright stood at the front of the class and put on her half-moon reading spectacles and cleared her throat.

'Now, children,' she said, peering at us over the rims of her spectacles. 'This was not an easy competition to judge, but I have come to a decision and when I announce the winner it is final and I don't want to hear one word out of any of you. Do you understand?'

Everybody in the class nodded their heads and that meant they understood. And then she announced the winner. And she said that the winner was me. And I didn't know where to look and Maggie turned from her seat at the front and threw me a dirty look and I thought her mum's should have won too, what with all those big words and fancy suggestions. I looked at Miss Bright and she told me to come to the front of the class when all I wanted to do was die and when I got to the front of the class I stared at my shoes and Miss Bright wrote the words to my song on the blackboard in big writing and then she made up a tune to my song and played it on the piano and sang my song out loud and that's when I noticed my shoelace was undone and I bent down and tied it straightaway.

Then Miss Bright said she was going to play my song again, only this time she'd only sing one line and, when she stopped, the class had to fill in the gap with the next line. And so she sang a line and when she stopped the class read the next line from the blackboard and then they sang it out loud. But I didn't need to look at the blackboard, 'cause I already knew the words.

It was my song.

The one about my da being quite musical

My da's da was a farmer and when my da was a wee boy he would get up at three o'clock every morning to muck out the byre before he went to school and if he didn't do it properly then his da would take the brush shaft and break it over his back to teach him a lesson he'd never forget. My da got the brush shaft regularly and not because he hadn't done a good enough job but just because his da was angry, about nothing in particular really, and when you're angry like that it makes you do cruel things like break brush shafts over wee boys' backs. My da's da was a cruel old man and it's no wonder my da grew into a cruel old man too.

My da's school was seven miles away and he walked there and back every day through fields and down dirt tracks and sometimes when he got to Billy Coyle's field he'd stop and pull up a turnip to break his fast. Billy never minded my da doing that, Christ, he only grew the turnips to feed the cows and the sheep through the winter anyway and sure Billy did the same thing himself when he was a wee boy walking to the same school my da was walking to now.

By the time my da got to school he'd already be tired from mucking out the byre and the seven-mile hike and maybe that's why he hated school so much, but he was good at arithmetic and music and he dreamed that one day he'd join the school choir. On Tuesdays, after school, he used to hang back in the playground under the open window of the music room and listen to the choir rehearse and if he knew the words he'd sing along. My da loved it when the choir sang 'Ave Maria' but he didn't know the words so he made them up as he went along and when he mucked out the byre in the mornings he'd sing his own version of 'Ave Maria' and the cows didn't seem to mind. And those Tuesday nights my da hung back in the playground under the open window made him late back to the farm for the afternoon milking and when he finally did get home his da would get the brush shaft out and, before he knew it, my da was nursing a sore back again.

He got the brush shaft so often for being late home on Tuesdays, that he came to associate music with pain. Later on when he was a grown man and drinking hard, he'd sing and it hurt him and he'd sing sad songs about falling to pieces with Patsy Cline on the radio and his heart was left with an emptiness that he'd fill up again with whisky night after night. Singing and drinking and pain, they went hand in hand.

My da was dying to join that choir but he kept it to himself for fear of being called a big Jessie by his six brothers and sisters. Months went by and he was practising and practising in that byre night and day until finally the desire to join the choir became too much and that's when he decided he was going to go and talk to Mr McCorgill the music teacher if it was the last thing he did. And so he went to the staff room the next morning and knocked on the door. His heart was pounding and his mouth was dry and he was worried Mr McCorgill might ask him to sing something right there on the spot and there he was having to peel his tongue from the roof of his mouth just to speak. The door opened and Mr McCorgill's huge frame filled the space where the door had been and my da suddenly felt out of his depth in the presence of this great maestro. Mr McCorgill looked at my da standing there with the arse hanging out of his trousers and his elbows poking through the sleeves of his jumper until my da cleared his throat and managed to find his voice and he asked Mr McCorgill if he could join his choir. Mr McCorgill looked down his nose and through his bifocals at my da and asked him, 'What's your name, son?'

'It's Joe. My name's Joe.'

'Right, Joe, can you sing?'

'Aye, I can sing right enough, Mr McCorgill. I've been

practising "Ave Maria" morning and night in the byre with the cows.'

'Right, I see. Well, I'll have to hear you sing, son. You can come to choir practice next Tuesday at four o'clock after school and we'll hear what you can do. All right?'

My da was trembling with the excitement. An appointment with the music teacher at four o'clock the following Tuesday! He couldn't believe his luck and he let his imagination run away with him and before he knew it he was famous the world over, with his own TV show called *Let Big Joe Entertain You*. He could see it all now: his name up in lights, women queuing to get his autograph, shiny new suits, one of those ruffle shirts, and maybe a velvet bow tie. The byre and the brush shafts would be tortures of the past. He looked back at the teacher. 'Thanks, Mr McCorgill, you won't regret it. I'll see you next Tuesday then.'

'Okay, son, and before I forget, you have to wear a white shirt to the choir.'

And my da stood there with the arse hanging out of his trousers and his elbows poking through the sleeves of his jumper and he swallowed hard and salty tears moistened the corners of his eyes.

'But I havenae got a white shirt, Mr McCorgill,' he said, looking at the floor and shuffling from foot to foot.

'I'm sorry, Joe. Nae white shirt, nae choir. That's the rules. Can your mother not buy you one, son? I see they have them on special down at O'Donnelly's haberdashery.'

'No, sir, my mother cannae buy me one. I've got six brothers and sisters and we eat turnip for breakfast.'

'Right, I see. Well, just see what you can do, Joe.'

'Aye, I'll see what I can do, Mr McCorgill.'

But my da knew that there was nothing he could do and with his heart heavy and his head hung low he headed for home. With his hopes of joining the choir now dashed, the lights in his name went out one by one and not even the thought of the brush shaft across his back for being late could speed him home. As he dragged his body the last few hundred yards in the seven-mile hike he didn't care if his da battered him to death with that fucking brush shaft.

A life without singing wasn't worth living anyway.

Even though my da never got to join the school choir he's still a brilliant singer, you can ask anybody. And my brother Andrew's a talented singer too. I think Andrew takes it off my da – 'cause it's certainly not off Mum. Mum couldn't sing to save herself, although she did the backing vocals on one of Andrew's new songs recently and funnily enough it sounded brilliant. Andrew said it's amazing what you can do with technology these days.

My da would have loved to have been a professional singer and to have lived his life on the stage and to have women throw their pants at him. But none of that ever happened and instead all my da ever knew was getting up early and driving his lorry every day and drinking a bottle of scotch and shouting at us at the end of every night.

When we were young we dreamed about what it would have been like if my da had been famous and we reckoned we'd probably have been the envy of our school and whenever the teacher went around the class asking everybody, 'And what does your daddy do?' we'd have stood up and said, 'Oor da's an entertainer, Miss.' And all the other weans in the class would have looked at us in awe and when it came their turn to stand up, all they would have been able to say was, 'Oor da drives a lorry, Miss,' or 'Oor da digs holes in the road, Miss,' or 'Oor da disnae have a job, Miss.'

My da's favourite singer was Neil Diamond and we loved Neil Diamond too. We used to put on his LP records every day and sing along to them when my da wasn't home and we'd shut our eyes as we sang and it was just like having Neil Diamond right there in our living room beside us. Sometimes we used to wish that Neil Diamond was our da – and Neil Diamond had that much money, Mum said, sometimes she wished he was our da too.

My da became well known for miles around for his singing and whenever he went to parties people would say, 'Come on Joe, gie us a song!' Only too happy to oblige he'd close his eyes and sing them a Neil Diamond number, sometimes the one that goes on about you being the sun and me being the moon, and everybody at the party would close their eyes too and listen to my da. When he finished everybody would tell my da he was pure brilliant and some would say my da sang the songs better than Neil Diamond himself ever could in a month of Sundays.

And, of course, my da loved to hear praise like that but sometimes it made him sad too and the sadness would set him off dreaming about what could have been and how he never made it to the big time and how he never got to stand on stage wearing a white ruffled shirt and a black velvet bow tie and sometimes Mum said that's why he drank so much, 'cause he was living a life of regret. Other times she said he drank so much 'cause he was a prick.

Once, on my da's birthday, we bought him a white ruffled shirt and a black velvet bow tie and when he saw them his face lit up and he put them on straightaway and then he picked up the hairbrush and closed his eyes and sang 'Cracklin' Rosie' and when he got to the chorus, we all sang along with him. And in some ways it made me sad to see my da so happy 'cause I wished I could have seen him happy like that more often.

And surely seeing your da happy now and again isn't too much to ask.

The milk round

My da didn't so much want to have children as breed workers.

Back in the old days when people put their empties out at night with the cat and had their milk delivered in the early hours, my da worked out that there was a way to make money while he slept. So he went out and bought a milk run and we ran it, while he slept.

Me and Mum and Izzy and Andrew would get up at half past three in the morning without making a sound for fear of waking him and we'd huddle around the gas fire in the kitchen, chittering with the cold and wishing we could go back to bed like normal people. Andrew said his pal John Brown's mum took him a cup of tea in his bed every morning before school and then Andrew asked Mum why we couldn't have a life like that and Mum told Andrew to stop moaning and to get outside and see if the diesel had frozen in the lorry or she'd give him a crack in the arse.

Sometimes if it was cold enough the diesel would freeze in the tank and if that happened Andrew would gather up some kindling sticks and place them on the ground underneath the fuel tank, then set fire to them and wait for the diesel in the tank to defrost. Once it was melted he'd put out the fire and run back inside the house to thaw out his frozen fingers in front of the gas fire.

We delivered the milk every morning of the week before we went to school and we used to collect the money every Friday night. One Friday night the rain had come on heavy and our feet were squelching in our shoes so Mum stopped in at the fish market and got a couple of empty polystyrene fish boxes and cut insoles out of them to put in our shoes. They helped to keep our feet warmer and a bit drier all right, only our feet stank of smoked haddock for a fortnight.

One Friday night, me and Izzy and Andrew were huddled together in the back of the van as we waited for Mum to drive to the next street so we could collect the money. It was freezing that night. The snow was turning to sleet and it blew straight into the back of the van 'cause there are no back doors on milk vans so it's easier to jump in and out as you deliver the milk to those who sleep.

'No' long noo,' Mum yelled out above the noise of the engine. 'We'll just finish up these last couple of streets and we'll soon be hame havin' a nice cuppa tea and a sausage. Hang on!'

So we held on, singing 'Cracklin' Rosie', and Andrew grabbed an empty milk bottle and pretended it was his microphone and he thought he was just like Neil Diamond and we told him his singing was shite, but he didn't care and sang all the more. He even did the actions.

As we pulled into Greenhills Crescent, Mum pulled on the handbrake and turned from the front seat to make sure we knew which doors we were going to knock on. The sight of the three of us frozen like snotters in the corner broke her heart.

'That's fuckin' it,' she said as she thought about my da toasting his arse at the log fire in The Village Tavern. She told us to get up the front beside her and we did. It wasn't much warmer but at least we were close to her and that made us feel better straightaway. Izzy and I perched ourselves on the passenger seat and Andrew sat at Mum's feet and clamped himself to her left leg making it nigh on impossible for Mum to change the gears.

'That's it for the night,' she said angrily, still thinking about my da toasting his arse, 'let's get hame, and get those sausages in the pan!'

We couldn't wait and our mouths watered as we set off down the dual carriageway through the sleet and in the direction of home.

'Mum, have we got any HP sauce in the hoose?' Izzy asked above the roar of the engine.

'We have indeed, Izzy!' she yelled back, her own saliva

starting to flow at the thought. 'We've even half a jar of pickled onions!' And we let out squeals of delight 'cause all of us loved pickled onions, especially if we were having a sausage.

We raced through the sleet as best we could in our beat-up old Transit van and Andrew broke into a wee song, the one he used to sing at the cub scouts and we all knew it, we'd been singing it for years, so we all joined in having a great old time when suddenly out of nowhere a car came up behind us with its headlights on full beam like it was searching for something and the headlights found the four of us huddled together in the front of the van. We narrowed our eyes, wincing into the glare, and I looked at Mum and she looked scared and dropped a gear with a crunch to slow the van down a bit.

'Maybe they want to pass us,' Mum said, adjusting her rear-view mirror to get a better look as we kept rolling slowly along and the car behind us got closer and closer and that's when we saw it was my da. Mum pulled over and he pulled in behind us and Mum told him we were heading for home and that's when the shouting started with my da asking Mum who she thought she was heading for home when we hadn't finished collecting in all the money and Mum told him that we were cold and hungry and that she didn't want to keep us out on a night as freezing as it was. And my da told Mum that she'd better get all the money in tonight or else there'd be trouble and we listened to everything that was going on and all we wanted to do was go home and have a sausage with HP sauce and a pickled onion if there were any left, and Mum said there was and we believed everything she told us.

And so my da stormed off and got back into his warm car with the walnut dashboard and headed back to his roaring log fire and toasty arse. Mum was sick to the stomach and if there was anywhere she could have taken us that night to get away from him she would have, and so with tears in her eyes she turned towards us and did her best to sound like everything was fine.

'Come on, let's go back and get the rest of that money in, eh? Then we'll get our sausages,' she whispered, and we knew that she was sad. Before we set off, she took the shoes off each of us and checked the polystyrene insoles to make sure our feet weren't too wet and then we did a U-turn across the dual carriageway and headed back to finish getting my da's money in. And she tried to get us to sing that wee song again. 'What was it again, Andrew? Come on, son, you know it's my favourite, let's hear it – you've a lovely voice.' And Andrew started to sing it again. Slowly we all joined in but with less gusto than before and the van moved at a snail's pace through the sleet and drivers behind us blew their horns in anger as we set off back up the dual carriageway.

I went and sat in the back of the van by myself and I watched the road as it rolled away from me like a giant conveyor belt and it seemed to me that that was how life was, one big conveyor belt rolling beneath you and once you're on that belt, it's hard to get off.

And as I watched the road roll away from me I thought about the sausages and the HP sauce and the pickled onions we'd have when we finally got home and then I closed my eyes and I wished my da would have stayed with us in the van and told Mum he loved her and maybe sung us one of his Neil Diamond songs or 'Ave Maria', but he didn't. So I had no choice but to imagine myself putting a sawn-off shotgun into his mouth and pulling the trigger and I smiled to myself and felt hopeful for the future.

If you've got leaving on your mind

She was wearing a blue-and-gold headscarf and a red brushed-nylon coat that tied in the middle and felt warm and soft to the touch. It was four o'clock already and as I ran out of school it was starting to get dark, 'dark o'clock,' Mum used to say. When I got to the school gates I was surprised to see my da there too and I looked at Mum in her red coat and her headscarf tied tight around her ears and my heart sank when I saw she wasn't smiling.

I couldn't think why my da would be there 'cause he was never there to pick us up at four o'clock, but I hadn't the mind to think about him when I saw her so sad. I ran across to Mum, my mind racing, not understanding, and Izzy and Andrew were there too by now and I think somebody took my hand, I'm not sure, and even now I don't like to remember it. Then Mum bent down and spoke to us. She gave me a kiss and next I knew she was walking away in the opposite direction to us and I was being dragged along by somebody's hand. I turned around to look at Mum one last time but she had her back to us, and as she walked away with her face to the wind I knew that she was crying.

Whoever had my hand kept dragging me and I gave myself a sore neck trying to turn around to try to catch another glimpse of Mum until I lost my footing and ended up dangling at the end of this hand. But I got my one last look at Mum and I stared at her for a few seconds, focusing with all the strength I had, not wanting her ever to disappear, but before I knew it she was just a red brushed-nylon dot in the distance. My eyes welled up and magnified the dot for a second before the tears spilled over and ran down my cheeks and the very next moment the darkness ate her up and all we were left with was him.

When we got older we knew why Mum'd had to leave and it wasn't just about getting the milk money in on a Friday night. He'd hit her around a few times too and once half her face was black and blue and she said she walked into the door and I believed her. I believed everything she told us. I looked at that door for a long time after and wondered how a door so flat could cause so much damage and I didn't think for a minute she was lying. I can still see that door now, as clear as day, the dimpled glass, the double security lock, the white gloss paint with the runs in it. Mum wore dark glasses for days til the swelling went down and Izzy said she looked just like Jackie-O on the telly and I nodded and laughed though I didn't know who Jackie-O was.

Once before when my da hit Mum she went to the local police and, well, they wouldn't do anything. They just said it was a husband and wife affair and they didn't get involved in the likes of that. So there was nothing Mum could do and nowhere Mum could go, I mean, where can you go when you've three kids, four dogs, five cats and a donkey called Annie? When we got older Mum told us that sometimes the pain of living with him drove her to think about putting her head in the gas oven or even jumping off the Cartland Bridge, and that's one of the highest bridges in Europe. And so it was no wonder that she left that day. You'd have done the same.

'Right, come on you lot, let's get back to the hoose,' my da growled and headed towards the milk van while we followed. We climbed inside through the doors that weren't there and sat on the aluminium floor that was icy to the touch. Andrew dared me to lick it to see if my tongue would stick and the cold seeped up through our duffle coats and into our arses and nearly gave us piles. Mum always used to say, 'Don't sit on the cold floor of the van or you'll get piles.' I shut my eyes and imagined it was her driving us home now and not him and thought about how she'd put the two-bar electric fire on when we got home and we'd all race to thaw our arses out in front of it and push and shove each other out of the way in a game that mostly ended in tears and always in burnt arses.

My da pulled the van in off the main road and parked it on the gravel driveway and we jumped out and headed towards the house. The place looked dark and empty. I thought that maybe she was inside, you know, sitting in the dark, 'cause there had been a power cut or something and that she was in there right now looking for the candles. I remembered the last time we had a power cut and one of our neighbours, Sonia, came to our door with a big box of candles that she had spare after she'd noticed our lights off for a long, long time. The next day we made a huge pot of mince and onion curry and took a big plate of it to Sonia and that was our way of saying thanks, without actually saying it, 'cause back in those days you didn't thank people for stuff, you just grunted in their general direction and then made them a mince and onion curry or a short-crust apple pie. Either way they'd be happy and grateful too, but as tradition dictated they didn't say thanks either. They just ate what was offered and gave you your plates and short-crust apple-pie dishes back clean.

We got inside the house and the worst was confirmed. Mum wasn't there. But Buster our pet boxer was and he stuck his wet nose up my school skirt and licked my arse and I knelt down and cuddled him and when I looked into his big brown eyes he sniffed at my face and licked my salty tears.

'Yir mither's gone,' my da said and we didn't say anything, just sat there on the green vinyl couch with our duffle coats on. The room was dark and cold and he put on one bar of the two-bar electric fire and heated his own arse at it and I looked at him and wished the hairs on his arse would catch fire.

Days passed, I don't know how many, I lost track. We went to school every day and every day we looked at the school gates at four o'clock just in case she'd be there again with her red brushed-nylon coat and blue-and-gold headscarf, but she never came. Sometimes I thought if I shut my eyes and wished hard enough when I opened them she'd be there, but Izzy said it didn't work like that and that we just had to be patient.

It seemed like an eternity since we last saw her. Then one day we came home from school and both bars of the electric fire were on and there was a big pot of mince and onion curry on the electric ring and me, Izzy and Andrew dropped our school bags and ran through the house calling her, desperate to see her, and as we ran through the living room I saw her red brushed-nylon coat slung across the arm of the green vinyl couch and I felt warm inside.

Nanny wears a beanie and Grampa joins the circus

She was Mum's mum and the kindest woman in the world. I never saw her consume anything other than tea and toast and I learnt her generosity by osmosis. Nanny was a market trader and the market lay down a cobbled laneway in the backstreets of Glasgow where hawkers and tinkers set up market stalls too and sold their wares regardless of the weather. It stank in the lane and it was dreich and dank but nothing would stop Nanny from going there 'cause she had her customers to attend to. So every day she put on her beanie and her winter coat and she went down the lane and that was that. The lane was full of drunk men who begged for money to buy whisky. I saw a sober man once and I was so surprised I asked Nanny, 'What's wrong with him?'

'He's sober, hen,' Nanny said, without missing a beat, while she rummaged through Jessie's cardigans and jumpers, four for a pound.

Nanny had a sixth sense for finding a bargain and she passed this glorious gift on to me and it doesn't matter where I go, I'll always find a bargain – like that time I found Cartier shoes at St Vincent de Paul for a few dollars, right next to a stunning Victorian damask bedspread they'd wanted five dollars for, but I knocked them down to three 'cause I have to get a bargain and there's nothing I can do about that. It's in my genes.

The other trait I've inherited from Nanny is wearing a beanie that closely resembles a tea cozy. Last time Mum came to visit me in Sydney, I wore my beanie to go shopping with her and she told me I looked daft. She's convinced I only wear it for a laugh. But the real reason is it reminds me of Nanny while it keeps me warm and it comforts me when I feel down.

Once when I was in the lane with Nanny I saw this drunk man begging. It was wet and cold and his trousers were in tatters and his shoes had no soles. He'd managed to beg enough to get himself some booze; I could see his wee quarter bottle of Cutty Sark sticking out of his back pocket. Nanny passed him by as he stood there in the wet and as she did she pulled out a couple of coins from the pocket of her winter coat and placed them discreetly in his outstretched hand. Jessie saw what Nanny did and called out to her from the other side of the lane, 'Haw, Nellie, he'll only buy drink wi' it!' And Nanny walked across to Jessie and leant across her table full of cardigans and jumpers, four for a pound, and whispered discreetly, 'I know he'll only buy booze wi' it, Jessie, but you tell me, what else does he have in his life?'

And Jessie didn't know what to say and so she shuffled from foot to foot and asked Nanny if she was interested in any of the nearly new bra and brief sets she'd just got in at two pound the set.

'Thanks, Jessie, but I'm not in the market for bras and briefs today. I'm looking out for a few jars of catering-size pickled gherkins for Maria the art teacher.'

'Try Whistling Tommy in the arcade, I think he just got a job lot in from that big hotel down there at the quay,' Jessie said. Nanny thanked her and made her way to Whistling Tommy and that's how it worked down the lane.

Nanny was married to Grampa and Grampa did everything Nanny told him. He even went to the chapel on a Sunday for the two of them and sometimes when me and Izzy and Andrew went to visit them on a Saturday night, Nanny would say to Grampa, 'Right, Bampsy!' – she always called him Bampsy – 'Get the potato pancakes on!' And so Grampa had to get into the kitchen and start peeling and grating potatoes and he had to follow the recipe Nanny's mum had handed down to her. Nanny's mum came from Lithuania where they make potato pancakes all day long, only they don't call them potato pancakes but they call them blinis, and what kind of a name is that?

Grampa's parents were Lithuanian too, and his dad

used to ride wild horses bareback on the prairies of Lithuania, just like in the Wild West movies you got on the telly on a Saturday afternoon. So Grampa grew up with a love of horses and ponies, but his da wouldn't let him ride them bareback on any prairies and was it any wonder that when he was still a wee boy he ran away from home and joined a travelling circus where he rode white horses bareback around the circus ring and children who came to the Saturday matinees screamed with excitement and delight?

One day a man came to the town where Grampa's circus was playing to make the first radio broadcast ever made from that little town. The broadcast would be made from the local swimming baths, 'cause that was the only building big enough to house the number of people who had shown up to see what was going on. The man in charge said he needed someone to jump into the swimming pool at the start of the broadcast so people for miles around could hear the splash through their radios in the comfort of their own homes. When the man asked for a volunteer Grampa stuck up his hand and the man said, 'Round of applause, please, for our volunteer!'

The crowd went mad as Grampa ran back to his circus caravan and put on his stripy swimming trunks then raced back to the pool and waited for his cue to jump. When it came Grampa took a run and a jump and he *splashed* into the water and half the pool emptied out, near enough soaking the man who was holding the microphone. The crowd went wild. When Grampa came back up to the surface of the water everyone was cheering and clapping for the man in the stripy swimming trunks who'd just made history in their little town. Grampa stood dripping at the side of the pool and his chest swelled with pride.

When Nanny and Grampa got married they had two sons, Chick and Bruce, as well as Mum, and when all three were grown up Bruce bought himself a wee car and that summer he drove Nanny and Grampa all the way from Scotland to Europe for a holiday and they toured all over and slept in a tent at bedtime. Grampa took his cine-camera and made movies of Nanny in the bulb fields in Amsterdam, at the Palace of Versailles, and at The Little Mermaid in Copenhagen. When they got back to Scotland, me, Izzy and Andrew watched the movie with Mum on Grampa's home projector screen and when we got to the bit with Nanny at The Little Mermaid, Mum started singing, 'Wonderful, wonderful, Co-pen-ha-gen!' and we all looked at Mum and then at each other and all of us thought she was mad. Years later Bruce had the movies put on a videotape to preserve the memories and I still have my copy of that video. It's more precious to me than anything else I own and I watch it in my quiet moments to see Nanny at the Palace of Versailles, waving at the camera like she's waving at me, and sometimes I wave back though I know it's daft, but I loved her so much, you see.

Uncle Chick and his flaking skin

Nanny and Grampa's son Chick had bad asthma and eczema too. And even when they were grown-up men, Chick and Bruce still lived at home with Nanny and Grampa. Chick used to work in the projection booth at The Roxy Cinema on the Glasgow Road and it was his job to make sure the films ran on time and there were no jumpy bits when he changed a reel. Mum said Chick had changed the reel the night my da took her to The Roxy to see *Psycho* on their first date.

We stayed at Nanny and Grampa's one Saturday night 'cause my da had taken Mum out for a fish supper and an advocaat and lemonade at The Welcome Inn at Ferniegair. Nanny had spoiled us with bags of sweeties from Lennox's, the sweetie shop at Bridgeton Cross, and later in the night she said the ice-cream van would be coming around too. I strained my ears to see if I could hear the chimes and as I strained I thought about what ice cream I was going to have then remembered one Saturday night when Bruce had just got back from the Swiss Alps and he went to the ice-cream van and got us an ice-cream cone with a chocolate Flake stuck in it. Bruce said that was called a '99' and he said he'd seen 99's in the ice-cream vans in the Swiss Alps. When we tasted them that night they tasted that good we wished Bruce would go away to the Swiss Alps more often. Next time Bruce was getting ready to leave for the Alps I asked him to bring me back a pair of Lederhosen just like the ones I'd seen the family Von Trapp wear in *The Sound of Music*. And sure enough, when Bruce got to the Alps he searched and searched in all the shops but there were no Lederhosen to be found. So he sent me a postcard and on it he wrote: *Keine Lederhosen hier*. I didn't know what that meant but when he came back without the Lederhosen, I knew what he had been trying to say.

Anyway, on the Sunday morning after the Saturday night we stayed at Nanny's, me, Izzy and Andrew got ourselves out of bed and put on our Sunday best. Me and Izzy wore our pink nylon dresses with the daisies around the bottom and the pearly buttons up the front and Izzy brushed her hair and tied it back and then she brushed mine too. Then we helped Andrew put on his grey trousers and his Fair Isle tank top that Nanny had got him from Jessie's stall at the market. Nanny made us two fried eggs each on toast and after our fried eggs Grampa said he would take us for a walk to Greenhall and buy us a choc-ice when we got there. When we were ready to go I tried to find Grampa to tell him it was time to get moving and from the kitchen I could see him out the back in his greenhouse watering his lemon-scented geraniums. I called out to him, 'Come on Grampa, are you ready?' and he held his hand up and showed me he was still smoking his Embassy Regal and I knew that meant he'd be out when he'd finished it and so I ran back to Izzy and Andrew and the three of us stood in the driveway at the front door and I kicked a stone around while we waited for Grampa to finish his smoke.

Nanny came to the front door, told us to enjoy our walk and handed Izzy Grampa's camera 'cause he wanted to take some pictures of the blue tits at Greenhall. Then Nanny said cheerio and climbed the stairs to the bedrooms to make the beds and that's when we heard her calling out Chick's name and Chick didn't answer. Then she called his name again and still he didn't answer. Nanny's voice got more frantic by the minute then we heard her try to open the door to Chick's bedroom and the blood-curdling scream she let out before falling to the floor.

I ran through the house and out the back to Grampa in his greenhouse, shouting for him to come quick, that Nanny was screaming, and Grampa raced in from the greenhouse and into the house and up those stairs three at a time. I followed him halfway up and when he got to Chick's bedroom he had to force the door open, and that's when he discovered Chick's dead body lying behind the door. Grampa could see that there was nothing to do 'cause Chick's face was already blue but Grampa knelt down beside him and tried to find a pulse though there was none to be found. Grampa reached out for Nanny and pulled her in close to him and Nanny was screaming and asking, 'God, Why? Why? Why?' Grampa tried to calm her as he yelled out for Bruce to run next door to Noreen's at number seven to use her phone to get an ambulance, 'cause Noreen was the only one in the street with the phone in. And then the pain got too much for Grampa too and that's when his own tears came and he pulled Chick's heavy body onto his lap and cradled him in his arms close to his heart, as if he was rocking him to sleep, and Nanny put her arms around Chick too and the three of them stayed like that for ages. Then Nanny kissed Chick on the forehead and she cried like any one of you would cry if it was one of your own.

And when I saw that I ran back down the stairs and out into the driveway and told Izzy and Andrew that something was wrong, that Chick's face was blue and he was lying in Nanny and Grampa's arms and that's when I said we should all run home to Mum. The three of us took off down Maitland Avenue and we didn't stop until we were halfway down Calder Street when Bruce pulled up beside us in his white Volkswagen Beetle, bundled us into the car and drove us the rest of the way home.

When we got there we raced into the house and Mum was standing with two rashers of streaky bacon in her hand and two fried eggs in the pan for my da's breakfast. Bruce told her straightaway that Chick was dead and Mum just stared at Bruce like she couldn't believe what she was hearing, then Bruce repeated it softly for her. That's when Mum dropped the two rashers of bacon onto the cold stone floor and fell back against the wall and slid down it until she was sitting on the cold stone floor herself. Bruce held me and Izzy by the hand and Andrew ran to Mum and Mum took him in her arms and started to sob for her brother Chick. She looked up at Bruce and she tried to be strong and keep the tears in, and in a half whisper she said to Bruce, 'Are you sure?' and Bruce said softly, 'Aye, hen, I'm sure.'

Mum didn't need to ask what had killed Chick. She thought of him taking his last breath in his bedroom that Sunday morning by himself then broke down and sobbed all the more and the four of us just stood there in the kitchen and looked at Mum and the two rashers of bacon on the cold stone floor and nobody knew what to say.

Years after Chick died, I'd think about him. In my mind's eye I can still see him in Nanny's kitchen with a towel over his head inhaling the steam from a bowl of hot water with eucalyptus oil in it, trying to get a breath. And I can see him on Nanny's red tartan couch in front of the gas fire with his trouserlegs rolled up to his knees, scratching the eczema on his shins until they bleed and the white flakes of dead skin are falling in a pile at his feet.

And now as I sit on my own couch in my living room in Sydney I sometimes roll up the legs of my trousers and scratch the eczema on my own shins and the soft white skin comes away in my fingernails and white flakes of dead skin fall in a pile at my feet too. And I think about Chick.

Christmas Day was always the worst

'Cause the pubs were shut all day it was the only day of the year that my da stayed home and it was the only day of the year we had to sit at the table with him and eat our dinner. Mum used to go and pick up Auntie Annie so she could come and have her Christmas dinner at our house, and Nanny, Grampa and Bruce would come too. And all of us wished the pubs would stay open all day long so we didn't have to sit at the same table as my da and every one of us wished it was over before it had even begun.

My da would start drinking early on Christmas morning and he'd sit in his leather chair by the gas fire with his whisky glass in his hand and he'd have that faraway look in his eyes he always had when he was drinking. When we gave him his present he'd reluctantly put his whisky glass down, take the present in his hands, feel it without opening it and then say something along the lines of 'another fuckin' jumper'. Then he'd throw the present back under the tree unopened.

Every Christmas was the same. Nervously we'd watch him out of the corners of our eyes as we went about the preparations for the dinner and we'd all have knots in our stomachs while we waited to see how he was going to behave that year. Once me and Andrew imagined what it would be like if Davey the milkman was our da and Andrew said he was sure Davey would like the presents we got him every year, well, at least he knew that Davey would open them. Then we imagined what kind of presents Davey would get us for Christmas. I said he'd probably get Andrew a soap on a rope from Marks & Spencer's and that he'd probably get me and Izzy talcum powder and bubble bath from the House of Fraser. Andrew said on Christmas morning Davey would wish us a merry Christmas and put on a Perry Como LP and we'd all sing and dance together in the good room and Mum would open the red crushed-velvet curtains and the brightness of the snow outside would rush in and dazzle our eyes and Davey wouldn't have to deliver the milk on Christmas Day, 'cause nobody's da delivers milk on Christmas Day.

Mum always got up early on Christmas morning to start preparing the dinner; we used to have brilliant dinners on Christmas Day. We always had two kinds of soup. Nanny would make the tomato, mince and rice soup and Mum would make the cock-a-leekie, and then we'd have boiled Brussel sprouts and carrots and potatoes mashed with a knob of real butter. One year, when Bruce came back from skiing in Italy, he brought back two bottles of Mateus Rosé and something called broccoli and he said that that's all they eat in Italy and I said what about spaghetti Bolognese and pizzas and Bruce said, 'Aye, all right, they eat spaghetti Bolognese and pizzas too.'

We always got a fresh turkey from Bobby's Chicken Shop on the Glasgow Road and every Christmas Mum bought a packet of Saxa turkey stuffing with sage, 'well, it is Christmas after all', and she'd fill the inside of the turkey with the stuffing and sometimes she'd put sausage meat inside the turkey too. Then she'd put the bird in the oven with a knob of butter on top and four hours later, when she brought it back out, it would be golden and crispy and we reckoned Mum made the best turkey in any house in the whole of the Glasgow Road.

One year my da said he wanted beef with string for his Christmas dinner. Mum said, 'Have you seen the price of it? And here's me still the balance of the turkey to pay.' And then my da said he didn't ask for much in life and it's a bad day when a man can't get beef with string when he has a notion for it. So Mum went to Peter Craig's, the butcher on the Glasgow Road, and she bought a joint of roast beef tied up with string and she roasted it in the oven for my da. That was the same year my da said all he wanted for Christmas was a pair of fur-lined boots and it's a bad day when a man can't get a pair of fur-lined boots when he has a notion for them. So Mum went out that same day and bought him a pair with the money she'd saved from the housekeeping and the night before Christmas she wrapped them up in a sheet of three-wise-men wrapping paper and put them under the tree. Next morning when my da got out of bed, Mum handed him his present and all of us were looking forward to seeing my da's face light up when he opened it. And after all that he just felt the parcel, said, 'pair of fuckin' fur-lined boots' and threw the present back under the tree unopened.

The best part about Christmas was the pudding. We always had two kinds of pudding. Bruce brought a Black Forest gateau and Mum would buy cream to pour all over it and before she poured it she'd say, 'Well it is Christmas after all.' And as if that wasn't brilliant enough, Mum used to make trifle and she put two cans of diced peaches in it and strawberry jelly and cold custard then topped it with two tubs of whipped cream from Lightbody's, the baker on the Glasgow Road. When it came time to have the pudding I could never decide which one to have first so I always had the two kinds of pudding on my plate at the same time and Mum used to say my eyes were bigger than my belly and sometimes she was right.

One year Mum invited one of Nanny's pals to come and join us for Christmas dinner and her name was Maria. She was an art teacher at The Church of Christ

High School and she was big and fat and Mum felt sorry for her 'cause she lived by herself with her fourteen cats and five dogs and Mum said nobody should have to be by themselves on Christmas Day. When Maria arrived that Christmas Day she couldn't believe her eyes when she saw the two soups, the turkey, the Brussel sprouts and the homemade trifle. Of course we knew my da wouldn't be happy about Maria coming for dinner 'cause she was big and fat and when I looked at my da out the corner of my eye he looked like a pot of milk about to boil over and all of us were waiting for the moment when his rage would escape and that's when I went under the table and thought about Davey the milkman again.

And then Mum shouted, 'Right, you lot, let's get started!' and I raced out from under the table. While I had been under there Mum had set the table and it looked pure brilliant. She'd put on the good white tablecloth with the blue embroidered forget-me-nots in the corners and the creases were still in it from when it was folded and put away the Christmas before. And on top of the good white table cloth she'd put an arrangement she'd made from the red plastic poinsettias and green plastic holly she'd bought, and she put skinny red candles in the middle of it like the skinny red candles you get on the front of Christmas cards sometimes. She'd set the table with two knives, two forks and two spoons for each of us and we had side plates and napkins folded up all fancy and sitting in the wine glasses. I sat next to Nanny and Grampa at the far end of the table away from my da and those eyes of his and all of us started with some soup. I had Nanny's tomato, rice and mince soup 'cause that's my very favourite and then I had some golden turkey, two Brussel sprouts and mashed potatoes and then Bruce told me I had to have some of the broccoli 'cause it would put hairs on my chest. I told him I didn't want hairs on my chest and if he liked it so much why didn't he eat it himself and that's when he laughed and uncorked the Mateus Rosé and poured everybody a glass.

My da didn't touch Bruce's wine, just sat at the head of the table and drank his whisky and ate his soup. He preferred Mum's cock-a-leekie to Nanny's tomato, mince and rice, and then he had some turkey and a Brussel sprout and all the while he was quiet and his eyes never left his plate and all of us were nervous, wondering what he was going to say this year and who was getting it first.

Just as Maria put the final mouthful of turkey into her mouth and laid her fork on the table my da told her to have some fuckin' Black Forest gateau. That's when all of our stomachs sank 'cause we knew that this was the start of it. Maria didn't really know where to look and then my da stood up and walked around to her place at the table and he took the soup ladle from the tomato, mince and rice soup and stuck it into the Black Forest gateau that Bruce had brought and then he splattered a huge ladle full of it onto Maria's plate. And I wanted to run under the table again and think about Davey the milkman but I didn't dare move and instead I stayed in my chair next to Nanny and Grampa and stared at the green Brussel sprout I'd left on my plate and didn't look up in case I was next.

Maria looked at my da and said, 'Thanks, Joe, but actually I don't eat cake. I don't like sweet food.' And my da said, 'How come you're such a big fat cow then?' and walked slowly away from the table and back to his leather chair. And nobody could look at Maria 'cause all of us were ashamed. Mind you, what my da had said was true, Maria was big and fat, but nobody deserves to be spoken to like that on Christmas Day. That's when Mum jumped up and started to clear the dishes away and everybody at the table helped and one by one we all left the dinner table and made our way to the kitchen with plates and bowls and glasses and cutlery and the nine of us ended up in the kitchen washing and drying dishes and wrapping up left-over turkey in tin foil and talking about the turkey curry Mum would make on Boxing Day. Bruce poured Auntie Annie another glass of Mateus Rosé and then she lifted her skirt and showed us her pink bloomers. And my da sat by himself in his leather chair by the gas fire drinking his whisky and staring into space with that faraway look in those eyes of his.

While we washed and dried we chatted and laughed and the dishes were done in jig time, then Auntie Annie said we should open up the Harvey's Bristol Cream and Nanny went to her bag and brought out the sherry glasses she'd brought from her china cabinet at home and Auntie Annie poured the sherries and me, Izzy and Andrew were allowed one too, well it was Christmas after all. As I sipped on mine I looked through the dimpled glass door of the kitchen and I saw that my da was fast asleep in his leather chair by the gas fire. I took another sip of my Harvey's Bristol Cream, closed my eyes and thanked God it was over for another year.

Andrew and Donald

Janet and Donald lived next door to us. They lived on one side of us and Sonia with the candles lived on the other. Janet and Donald didn't have any children of their own and Andrew and Donald got on like a house on fire, so Andrew became the son that Donald never had and Andrew loved Donald as much as Donald loved him.

One night when Mum was tucking Andrew into bed, Andrew asked Mum if Donald could be our da and Mum said it wasn't quite as simple as that and that he should go to sleep now, that it was late, and wee boys shouldn't be awake at this hour talking about replacement da's and God only knows what. It was only the week before that Andrew had asked if Davey the milkman could be our da, too. It seemed Andrew wanted any da except the one he had.

Donald had a huge back garden and he grew his own vegetables and berries there and he showed Andrew how to grow tatties. He told him how, if you pinched the wee white flowers off the plants, the tatties would grow bigger and he promised Andrew that once the tatties were the right size they'd build the biggest bonfire he'd ever seen and Andrew would get to wrap the tatties in tin foil and put them in the fire to bake them in their own skins and the two of them would enjoy them straight from the flames with a big knob of real butter each.

Andrew couldn't wait for the tatties to be big enough so they could build that bonfire and they checked the tattie plants together every day. Donald told Andrew when you pinch the flowers you should close your eyes and make a wish, so Andrew closed his eyes and wished for a new da and the biggest tatties the town had ever seen. And once he'd made his wish Andrew told Donald he was going to give the wee white flower to Janet, and Donald looked down at Andrew and his heart ached for the son he never had.

The time for digging up the tatties was fast approaching and all Andrew could talk about at home was Donald. Donald this and Donald that, Donald and the tatties, Donald and the bonfire. Mum was run ragged with all this talk about Donald every minute of every day and then, one Tuesday at five o'clock, Mum heard the drone of Donald's Morris Minor coming up Victoria Street and you couldn't see Andrew for dust as he flew up the driveway to Donald's back door like he did every day at five o'clock. He knocked on the door and waited and it was Janet who opened the door.

'Is Donald comin' oot to play, Janet?' Andrew asked.

'He's just coming in the front door now, son. Do you want to come in and wait?'

'No, I'll wait here for him,' Andrew said and he sat himself down on Donald's back step. Donald raced into the house through the front door and dropped his bag on the couch as he headed to the back door to see his wee pal, who was always waiting there at five o'clock when he got home.

'Hello, Andrew, son, you're here waiting for me already, eh?'

'Aye, Donald. Are you comin' oot to play?'

'You bet I am. Let's go and check the tatties, eh?'

'Aye, okay, Donald, and look, I've got a surprise for us.'

Andrew stretched out his wee hands and proudly displayed two knobs of butter wrapped in tin foil. 'It's for the tatties, Donald,' Andrew said. 'It's Lurpak butter, Donald – no' margarine.'

'What a treat, Andrew, son. We'd better get movin' and check on the tatties then, eh? Maybe tonight's the night!'

And with that they raced down the garden path to the tattie plants and Donald crouched down and scraped around in the dirt and started to smile. And Andrew crouched down too and they both turned their heads and looked straight at each other, nose to nose, and both of them were smiling.

'They're ready, aren't they, Donald?' Andrew said.

'Aye, son, I think they are. Tonight's the night! Let's get the spade and make a start – it's getting dark already. We'll be eating our tatties by moonlight!'

So Donald got the spade from his garage and dug up the first plant to reveal five of the biggest tatties Andrew had ever seen in his life.

'Ah, Donald, they're beauties!' Andrew shrieked.

'Aye, they are that, son, and all your own work. Did I no' tell you my secret about pinching the flowers and how that would make the tatties grow big like that?' Andrew nodded in agreement as Donald handed him the spade. It was nearly the same size as Andrew and Donald handed it to him and showed him how to put his wee foot on one side of it and how to push it in under the tattie plant and bring up the tatties without damaging them.

'That's the way, son,' Donald said proudly, watching over Andrew as he dug up his first tatties, 'you've really got the hang of it there.'

Andrew furrowed his brow in concentration and kept on digging and digging, showing Donald what a big man he was, and once the tatties were up they gathered up a collection of branches and sticks and started the fire. It didn't take long to catch and soon it crackled and roared while Andrew and Donald scrubbed the tatties under the outdoor tap, and Donald showed Andrew how to wrap them in tin foil and place them in the fire. Then Donald got his tartan travel rug from the boot of his Morris Minor and placed it close to the fire and Andrew and Donald sat together on the rug, just the two of them, looking into the flames and waiting for the tatties, and neither of them could have been any more contented. Their faces went pink from the heat as they stared into the flames and the flames mesmerised them as the smoke twisted and curled on its way up to the moon.

After half an hour Donald said the tatties were ready so he pulled them from the flames with a big long branch that he'd saved from the pile of firewood they'd collected. The tatties were black on the outside and when Donald cut them open the white powdery flesh looked fluffy like snow. Andrew popped one knob of butter on top of each and watched as it melted and trickled into the powdery flesh. He said they were the best tatties he had ever had, even better than the new season Golden Wonders Mum used to boil in their jackets. As the last flames of the fire died and the orange embers glowed Donald said it was probably time for Andrew to be getting home to bed. 'Come on, son, I'll walk you home,' he said tenderly.

But Andrew didn't want the night to end. He wanted to sit there with Donald all night long and ask him questions about tatties and fires but he knew he had to go. It was dark and late and the excitement of the tatties had left him exhausted.

Donald took Andrew's hand as they started down the path towards home and Andrew squeezed Donald's hand as much as his wee hand could squeeze a grown man's. He thought about the secret wish he'd made about having Donald as his new da and he wondered if it would ever come true, but Mum had told him before that life was never that simple.

Mum opened the door to the pair of them, their faces still pink from the fire and their fingers black and sooty from the tattie skins.

'Just returning your wee yin, Betty,' Donald said.

'Ach, thanks, Donald. Looks like you two have had a good time,' Mum said, 'and it looks like we might need to get the scrubbing brush to Andrew's fingernails!'

'Aye, he's a dirty wee bugger tonight, Betty,' Donald said as he kneeled down beside Andrew. 'Awright, wee man, time to say good night. We had a good time tonight, didn't we son?'

'Aye, we did, Donald. Will I see you again tomorrow then?'

'Of course you will, pal. I wouldn't miss that for the world – you just listen for my Morris Minor coming up Victoria Street at five o'clock and I'll meet you on my back step. But right now it's time for your bed.'

Donald smiled at Andrew, the son he never had but wished for with all his heart, and Andrew smiled at him, all black soot and grimy, and Donald put his arms around Andrew and cuddled him and he shut his eyes tight and a wee tear ran down the bridge of his nose as he whispered

'Good night, son' into Andrew's ear. And Andrew wrapped his arms around Donald's neck and pressed his wee pink cheek against Donald's and whispered back, 'Good night, da.'

Is that for your porridge or are you going to plant crocuses in it?

I used to go to the Brownies on a Tuesday night and I loved it there. One night Brown Owl divided us into different groups and each of these groups got the name of a bird: The Yellow Canaries, The Robin Red Breasts, The Little Brown Sparrows and The Blue Tits. I was in The Blue Tits and Mum said that was okay, 'cause out of all the birds the blue tits were the most beautiful, and I believed her.

The next week for homework we had to find a picture of our birds from newspapers and magazines, stick them down on a big piece of paper and bring them to the Brownies the next Tuesday. My grampa used to take photographs of birds so I asked him the next day if he had photographed any blue tits and he said he hadn't but he had photographed Auntie Annie's blue budgie in its cage and I said that would do 'cause who'd know what a blue tit looked like anyway?

I took my photograph and glued it down on a big sheet of blue paper and wrote blue tit at the bottom in blue pen. I thought my homework was pure brilliant and couldn't wait to see the other Brownies' faces when they saw how great it was too.

The Tuesday night eventually arrived and when I got to the Brownie hall I discovered all the other Brownies had done something called collages and they had stuck loads of pictures and clippings of information from the newspapers on what their birds ate and where they slept and how they fed their babies and all of them were colourful and sparkly and I didn't know where to look. I thought about saying I had left mine at home but knew they'd know I was lying and so I had no choice but to put mine on the table along with the rest of them, and then I went to the toilet and hoped when I came back it would all be over. As I made my way back from the toilet I saw Jean Rowntree from The Little Brown Sparrows looking at my blue tit and then she marched straight to Brown Owl and she whispered something into Brown Owl's ear and pointed at my picture.

'Ali,' Brown Owl said, 'is this your blue tit?'

'Yes it is, Brown Owl.'

'I've been having a look at it and I must say this is the first time I've seen a blue tit that looks almost identical to a blue budgerigar.'

'Is it, Brown Owl?'

'Yes, it is. And I was just wondering, what made you think this was a blue tit?'

I didn't know where to look so I said, 'The blue tit and the blue budgie are from the same family, Brown Owl.'

'Oh, really? And who told you this?'

'My grampa told me, Brown Owl.' Of course Grampa had said nothing of the sort but I had to blame somebody.

Brown Owl raised her eyebrows, picked up Jean Rowntree's brown sparrow collage and congratulated Jean on an excellent sparrow collage, perhaps *the most* excellent she had ever seen in all her years as a Brown Owl. Jean looked across at me and the way she looked at me got my back right up.

Once the bird collages were all put away, Brown Owl told us she had some special news, and that special news was there was going to be a Brownie camp and she hoped that all the Brownies would be able to attend. During that Brownie camp there were going to be opportunities to research your bird group as well as games and activities and I couldn't wait. Brown Owl gave us a list of essential camping items we would have to take with us and we had to show the list to our mums and report back the next week if we would be able to go or not.

I was so excited I ran all the way home to ask Mum if I could go. She said that I could and I showed Mum the list with 'one pair of sturdy walking shoes, one average-sized plastic breakfast bowl, one sleeping bag, one toothbrush, one bar of soap, one towel, several items of warm clothing, one knitted hat, one waterproof coat'. And I kept the list with me in my bed that night and couldn't sleep for wondering if any of my shoes were sturdy enough and what did they need to be sturdy for?

The day of the departure to camp arrived and Mum had prepared my bag with the essential camping items except I still didn't have my average-sized plastic breakfast bowl. It was already one o'clock and I had to be at the Brownie hall to board the mini bus at one-thirty. So Mum grabbed me by the hand and we raced down to the shops on the Glasgow Road to see what we could find and we couldn't find anything 'cause all the shops were closing for their half-day Wednesday trading. Just as we were about to give up hope of finding a shop still open, Mum noticed that the lights were still on in Joe Battersy's hardware shop and so we rushed inside just as Joe was heading to the door to turn the key in the lock.

'Ah, just in time, Betty. What can I do for you this afternoon?' Joe asked Mum.

'Well, it's a bit of an emergency, Joe – we need an average-sized plastic breakfast bowl for Ali here. She's just heading off on her Brownie camp and she needs it for her porridge in the morning.'

'Sorry, Betty, I don't carry plastic breakfast bowls these days, not since the Tuesday markets opened up in the car park at Hasty's Farm and they stock everything there from plastic breakfast bowls to imported polyester men's ankle socks at four pairs for a pound.'

My heart sank as I listened to Joe and I imagined the shame of being turned away from the mini bus for not having all the essential items from the list with me and then I thought maybe if I asked nicely, Brown Owl would still let me come if I promised not to eat any breakfast. Mum could see my disappointment. She took my hand and we turned and walked towards the big red door of Joe's hardware store and just as we were about to open the door Mum noticed Joe's display of crocus bulbs in the window and right next to the crocus bulbs there was a pile of big green plastic bulb bowls. She turned to Joe and said, 'Joe, I see you've lovely crocus bulb bowls in the window. How much are they?'

'They're one pound twenty each and they're big enough to hold a dozen and a half crocus bulbs, Betty. We've got hyacinth bulbs too, if you're interested, and the daffodils are coming in on Friday.'

'I'll take the bowl for now, Joe, but I don't need any bulbs just at the minute.'

'Okay, Betty, I'll wrap it up for you.'

'Don't worry, I'll just pop it into Ali's bag.' And I couldn't think what was going to be worse, showing up at the mini bus without an average-sized plastic bowl or showing up at the kitchen on the first morning of the

Brownie camp with a bowl that was designed to incubate a dozen and a half crocus bulbs.

'But, Mum, the list of essential items says, an *average-sized* plastic breakfast bowl and that crocus bowl is big enough to feed The Canaries, The Little Brown Sparrows, The Robin Red Breasts and The Blue Tits all at the same time!'

Mum told me to shut up and stop complaining and to remember that there were people starving in the world. I didn't see the connection but then with Mum there often wasn't one. So, rather than risk being ridiculed and ostracised by my Brownie pack for not going to the Brownie camp, I decided instead to risk being ridiculed and ostracised for showing up at the breakfast kitchen with a larger than average-sized plastic breakfast bowl.

With my crocus bowl pushed down as far as possible into my bag I boarded that mini bus and as we trundled out of the street we all sang Brownie songs and I tried to push thoughts of breakfast as far out of my mind as I possibly could.

I sat at the back of the bus just across from my pal Maggie and my other pal Susan and as we set off they brought out their breakfast bowls and Maggie's had Donald Duck on the side and Susan's had bunny rabbits running around the rim and when I thought about my crocus bowl, with 'Plant Use Only' stamped on the side, I got a terrible sinking feeling in the pit of my stomach.

Then Maggie and Susan asked me if they could see my breakfast bowl and I said, 'Och, mine is at the bottom of my bag and I'd have to take out my sturdy walking shoes to get at it. I'll show it to you when we get to the camp.' They seemed happy enough with that and me, I couldn't have been unhappier, and suddenly I wished I'd never boarded that mini bus and that I'd stayed at home with Mum and planted crocuses instead.

When we arrived at the camp, Tanya, the camp coordinator, showed us to our tents and then she showed us where to have a wash and where to show up for breakfast the next morning. As we toured the camp site my fears about the breakfast queue escalated from a terrible sinking feeling in the pit of my stomach to a frantic state of dread in my whole body. I started to imagine the breakfast line the next morning and I could see the queue of bubbly Brownies chatting excitedly about their sturdy walking shoes and admiring each other's bowls and next thing I know, beads of sweat are forming on my forehead and rolling down into my brown bushy eyebrows.

No longer able to contain the dread, I went inside my dark tent and sat on the wet grass and held my head in my hands and wept. I wept for Mum, the only person in the world who ever told me I was beautiful like a blue tit and the only person in the world who didn't care whether I ate my breakfast from a crocus bowl or if I ate any breakfast at all. One of the Brownies heard me crying and she went and told the Brownie Commissioner who was Brown Owl's boss, and the Commissioner came straightaway and asked me if I was okay. Of course I couldn't tell her about the shame of my crocus bowl so instead I told her I was missing my mammy and that I didn't know if I could get through the night sleeping in that tent without her. And then the weeping got worse and all the Brownies from the other tents gathered at the flap of my tent and peered in to see who would be making such a disgrace of herself on their first trip away from home without their mammy. When they saw it was me they put their heads together and whispered to each other and I knew they were asking questions about my breakfast bowl and they were saying how it seemed strange I hadn't wanted to show mine on the bus and so I told the Commissioner I wanted to go home and the Commissioner told me, 'Come come, there's no need to be going home. You've only been here two hours and what's everybody going to think of you if you head home without even sleeping one night in the great outdoors?'

But how could I tell her my fear of what people thought of me for going home without even sleeping one night in the great outdoors was nothing compared to my fear of someone in the breakfast queue asking me, 'Is that for your porridge or are you going to plant crocuses in it?' And so I sobbed even more and then the sobbing turned into wailing until the Commissioner knew she had no choice but to agree to drive me home before all of the other Brownies started wailing for their mammies too. So with my head hung low, I dragged my bag of essential camping items through the wet grass behind me to the Commissioner's car and didn't dare look up from the grass for fear that the Brownies would be staring at me and whispering in each other's ears about the Brownie from The Blue Tits who's missing her mammy.

The sun was almost set for the night and the darkness wasn't far away as me and the Commissioner drove up the dirt track and out of the Brownie camp. Just before we turned right onto the sealed road that would take us to the motorway, I turned back and looked one last time at the camp. Each of the tents had its own oil lamp burning outside and I could see the Brownies in their sturdy shoes sitting around the orangey flames of the camp fire telling each other stories and all sorts of lies about their breakfast bowls and how they weren't missing their mammies one little bit, and me, I just turned my head in the direction of home and watched the dusky hills roll past as the rhythm of the Commissioner's car rocked me gently to sleep.

Vladimir's deli and my bare arse

I used to think Mum drank the vinegar straight from the gherkin jar 'cause her grandparents were Lithuanian. Once the last gherkin in the jar had been eaten, Mum used to lift the jar to her mouth and gulp down its contents using her teeth as a sieve for the pickling spices and the long bits of stringy dill that floated in amongst the gherkins. Lithuania is right next door to Poland and we grew up on Polish gherkins and Polish sour-dough bread and Polish pork ring sausages and we used to get them once a week from Vladimir's delicatessen at the Gorbals.

We didn't have a telly back then or Monopoly or Scrabble or Buckaroo like our cousin David had and so for a laugh sometimes I'd lift my skirt and run through the living room exposing my bare arse to Mum and Izzy and Andrew. And then one day Mum came up with a new game that involved cutting off the little knot of skin that tied the two ends of the pork sausage together to keep it in its ring shape. Then she'd keep it in her pocket and when I exposed my arse again she'd grab me and stick the little knot between the cheeks of my arse as I ran past. The first time it happened, I didn't like the new game very much, but Mum and Izzy and Andrew thought it was the best game they'd ever played. Buster loved this new game too 'cause it meant he would get the knot of sausage skin as a treat at the end, so when the game started Buster joined in enthusiastically, running after me and sniffing and licking my arse, searching for the treat. Sometimes even when I wasn't exposing my arse and just minding my own business, Mum and Izzy and Andrew would tease Buster and give him orders like, 'Get the pork ring, boy, get the pork ring!' and Buster would run after me, salivating at the thought of the tasty morsel he might find.

As time went on, having the dog run after me trying to lick my arse every minute of the day lost its appeal and so I turned my attention to other ways of passing my time which meant me keeping my knickers up and my skirt down and life became very dull. And just when I thought things couldn't get any duller, I became vegetarian and Mum seemed to respect that if I didn't want to eat meat, then I certainly didn't want to have pieces of pork sausage stuck up my arse and so she let me be, although not before considering nut cutlets and lentil rissoles as vegetarian alternatives.

With my arse now covered up at all times, Mum

continued on her weekly trips to Vladimir's Deli to stock up on jars of gherkins and pork ring sausages and although I still went with her I stayed in the car, my new vegetarian principles preventing me from entering any establishment that sold dead animals. On the way home, though, I'd sit in the back seat of the car with my buttocks firmly clenched, one eye on the jar of gherkins and the other on the pork ring sausages sticking out of the brown paper bag laughing at me.

I think back to those days with enormous fondness yet the memories are tinged with a certain sadness, for exposing my arse had become my signature tune as it were, something I had identified with so strongly and for so long. And today, as I pass the delicatessen counter in the supermarket my buttocks clench in conditioned response to past traumas and the desire to lift my skirt to the waist and go running through the meat section exposing my arse overwhelms me.

And of course I blame my mother for all of this and some day when I'm old and can no longer contain my urges I'll be rugby tackled by a security guard in the supermarket, the police will be called and I'll be frog-marched to the manager's office and charged with indecent exposure.

Freud would have a field day.

Right there in God's house for Chrissake

Beatrice the Brown Owl had warned us if we wanted to graduate some day from the Brownies to the Girl Guides then we had to be in church every Sunday at one o'clock and right away I got concerned 'cause that's when my favourite TV show, *Randall and Hopkirk (Deceased)* came on telly. *Randall and Hopkirk (Deceased)* was about a detective agency and had two detectives in it – one called Randall and the other called Hopkirk. One day Hopkirk is murdered and Randall is left alone to solve the crimes. Then, out of the blue, Hopkirk reappears as a ghost wearing a white suit and he sits on Randall's desk and helps him solve all the mysteries and crimes that come up. So, the way I saw it, *Randall and Hopkirk (Deceased)* was in a way about God and the church and everything, what with Hopkirk having died yet still able to come back from the dead, and I was sure it was on at this prime time so that all good Christians could take faith in the fact that there was some kind of life after death and that you could still come back from the dead and appear on the telly and maybe help solve the odd crime or two if you had a mind to.

In the end I decided I'd better go to church after all 'cause something told me Brownies shouldn't be having thoughts of putting sawn-off shotguns into their daddies' mouths, and so at quarter to one the following Sunday, I put on my red vinyl Sunday coat and made the trip to church by foot. The service was long and I fidgeted in the pew and picked the skin from around my fingers till they bled and just when I thought I couldn't take another moment of the boredom the minister announced how he looked forward to seeing us all again next week.

You fuckin' beauty, I thought, desperate to get out of there and get home and get the telly on, thinking maybe if I was lucky I'd catch the end of *Randall and Hopkirk (Deceased)*. I started shuffling out of the pew only to be rooted to the spot the very next moment as the minister announced, 'All Brownies should now proceed to the church hall for the Sunday school.'

'You're fuckin' kidding me,' I thought to myself as I dragged my body through the vestibule and into the Sunday school hall for another hour of drudgery. The other Brownies were in the church hall too and chatted excitedly amongst themselves about the different points the minister had raised during the sermon. As for me, I could only think about *Randall and Hopkirk (Deceased)*. We had to break into different groups and I hated it when you had to do that 'cause I just wanted to stay with my best pal Maggie. We sat around in our groups and listened to some story about Jesus and Mary, then we sang a few songs about envy, jealousy, malice and spite, and after that we had to listen to this fat guy with a beard tell us how these emotions must never be allowed to reside in our hearts and I wondered what reside meant for a moment then went back to thinking about *Randall and Hopkirk (Deceased)*.

Finally, the bell rang signalling the end of the torture. I jumped from my seat, grabbed my wee red vinyl coat from the bottom of the pile of coats, toppling all the others above it to the floor, and ran for the door. I was free and I ran and I ran all the way home not even stopping to put on my wee red vinyl coat, instead holding it high above my head letting the wind catch it. The sun shone through it and I felt its pink rays on my face and I felt safe right there under my coat. I made up my mind right there and then that that would be the last time I would ever give up the telly for the church. The two just didn't compare.

Mum's big knob

The minister's wife was Beatrice, the Brown Owl for our Brownie pack, and one night she announced she needed an assistant and that assistant would be the Tawny Owl, not as important as the Brown Owl, but still an important role that not just anybody could fill. And so I ran home that night after we sang 'The Lord's Prayer' and asked Mum if she would be the Tawny Owl and Mum told me to fuck off, that she had enough to do, what with my da and his drinking, me, Izzy and Andrew, four dogs, five cats and a donkey called Annie to contend with. But I pleaded and pleaded and eventually she came over to meet the Brown Owl and she got the job and I was delighted, even though some of the Brownies got confused and thought that Tawny Owl meant that Mum's name was Tony and went on to call her Tony for their entire Brownie lifetimes.

Mum and Beatrice started to become friends, which surprised us because Beatrice's husband Adam was the minister and we couldn't think what they'd want hanging around with people like us who didn't care much about God. At first Beatrice just came to our place by herself, then she started bringing Adam around as well and we thought maybe they were trying to help us find God or something, but Mum said they had probably never experienced anything like us before and were intrigued to see how the other half lived. 'We're not rich,' Mum used to say, 'but we do see life.'

Adam used to come round and spend a lot of time in the good room with my da with the door closed tight, and we thought maybe Adam was trying to convert my da. He used to come to our place carrying a plastic bag with Tennent's Lager printed on the side and shortly after arriving and chatting to us in the kitchen he would excuse himself, make the sign of the cross above our heads, and head to the good room where my da would be drinking himself into oblivion with the telly Mum had just bought from Big Marion's Second Hand Bargains on the Glasgow Road blaring in the corner. As he made his way towards the good room Adam's Tennent's Lager bag made strange clinking noises, which we put down to bottles of holy water he must carry about with him in case of one of those holy emergencies ministers sometimes have.

One night Mum invited Adam and Beatrice around to have a bite to eat and a glass of Mateus Rosé and of course they came and Adam brought his Tennent's Lager carrier bag with the strange clinking noises and as the night wore on, the drinks, the nibbles and the conversation started to dry up and it became apparent to everybody, except Beatrice and Adam, that they had overstayed their welcome. And so without any warning my da put his glass down, stood up from the couch, peeled off his shirt, vest, trousers and underpants, dropped them onto the carpet and announced that he was off to bed, and duly walked out of the good room wearing nothing but his socks. Beatrice and Adam didn't flinch but Mum, well she was so embarrassed she tried to draw attention away from the situation and started talking really fast and loud about the new telly she'd bought from Big Marion's Second Hand Bargains on the Glasgow Road. And as Mum spoke, she stood up and ran her hand over the lovely wooden-veneer cabinet, urging Beatrice and Adam to take note of the absence of any scratches and, without pausing for breath, she moved straight onto a demonstration of the lovely big knob that was just the right size for changing channels. She gave them a demonstration of each of the channels too, although it was late and the telly had finished for the night, so all they got was snow in various frequencies.

Adam didn't come around so much after father dropped his trousers like that, but Beatrice seemed to come all the more.

Having chosen the telly over God my red vinyl coat didn't see the light of day much, so Mum decided we should at least go to church once a year on Christmas Eve. The service started about eleven and ran through until just after midnight and we were always glad to go on that one night 'cause it made Christmas feel all Christmassy. I got to wear my red vinyl coat and when we got back to the house we'd crack open a bottle of Harvey's Bristol Cream Sherry and open one present each from under the tree. Mind you, the worst part about the Christmas Eve service was that just as the clock struck midnight in the church, Adam would stand in his pulpit and instruct everyone to turn to the person sitting next to them and shake their hand and wish them a very merry Christmas. The first time he told us to do that I thought, 'You've got to be fuckin' kidding me, I don't even know the prick sitting next to me.' Of course, it was all right for Adam up there in his pulpit removed from the masses but I wondered how he'd like it, down here in the pews, having to wish a merry Christmas to people he had never met. That's the trouble with the church, it's so insincere. Anyway, year in, year out I clenched my teeth and my buttocks and I'd get through that bit. After all, it was only once a year.

The last Christmas we would ever set foot inside that church my red vinyl coat barely fitted me anymore. Adam was up there in his pulpit going on about Jesus, a big star, and three wise guys bearing gifts nobody could spell, and just as it was approaching midnight and getting close to that bit where he was going to make us turn to the person next to us and wish them and their families a very safe, holy and merry Christmas, there came this huge crash on the outside door of the church. The entire congregation looked in horror towards the door and the crash came again and there was a great sense of unease right there in God's house.

Everybody stared at the door wondering what was going to happen next and I looked at Adam and he was staring at the door as well and his nose glowed red in the candle light. The sound came from the door again – BANG, BANG, BANG! – and people in that congregation started to stand up nervously and were turning to face the door. Whoever was out there was determined to get in and just kept on banging and banging and then pushing that door until finally the massive door to God's house burst open and in fell my da, flat on his face in the middle of the aisle, pissed out of his mind, a fresh fall of snowflakes adorning his crown.

We didn't want to believe what we were seeing but unfortunately the evidence was right there in front of us on the floor of the church. The entire congregation gasped in unison and stared in disbelief at such a display on holy ground as my da managed by some miracle to get himself to his feet and stay upright long enough to grab onto a pew. As he stood there, wobbling to and fro, he saw Adam in the pulpit in his dog collar and purple gown and he didn't seem to recognise him at first. Then you could see the realisation dawn on him that the bloke up there in the purple get-up was Adam, his 'auld china' by the way. Adam, normally creative in times of need, glanced around the congregation, his eyes greedily searching for a television set with a scratch-free veneer and a big knob, but there was none to be seen. And all eyes were on Adam as my da, swaying on his feet, managed to get a sentence together.

'Hey, Adam – is that you, pal? It's me, Joe – yir auld china! I went to your place, pal, but you wurny there. Just wondered if you fancied a wee dram like? What time do you knock off your shift, by the way?'

The colour drained from Adam's face and he sent a silent prayer to the Lord promising if He could open up the ground right now and let him disappear into the black hole of eternity, then he'd truly believe in His greatness and would worship and spread the holy word without ever touching another drop of Johnny Walker. Then he closed his eyes and waited for the miracle to happen. When he opened them again, nothing had changed. My da was still there in the aisle waiting for an answer to his question and the rest of the congregation held their breaths for Adam's response. Mustering up as much holiness as he could find, Adam took a deep breath and made his way from the pulpit towards my da in the aisle. And he went up to him as if he didn't know him and guided him to a seat on one of the pews at the front, like you might a lost sheep who has strayed from the fold, and he whispered into my da's ear for him to sit there and keep quiet until he'd finished his shift, then they'd get that drink. Then Adam made the sign of the cross above my da's head and headed back to the pulpit feeling holier than thou.

Obligingly, my da sat down, folded his arms in front of himself and fell asleep right there in the very front row of God's house. Adam looked down on him from on high and raised his eyes to Heaven and paid thanks to the Lord for this small miracle. And then, guess what? Another miracle! In all the confusion Adam forgot where we were up to in the proceedings and wished us all a very merry Christmas and asked us all to keep an open heart to those less fortunate than us and we knew he was talking about my da in the front row. Then he said something about the Sunday school this coming Sunday, bade us good night and a moment later he was gone through a side door. We didn't have to shake our good neighbours' hands and wish them and their families a very safe and merry Christmas! I couldn't have asked for any better gift than this one Adam had unknowingly bestowed upon us. And to think I had my da to thank for that.

The Lord truly works in mysterious ways, I thought as we headed home to crack open a bottle of Harvey's Bristol Cream Sherry and open one present each from the bottom of the tree. Just as we got home the snow started to come down heavy and Mum drew the big red crushed-velvet curtains to try to keep the heat in and we wondered what state my da would be in when he'd finally get home.

Then I put the telly on. As if it hadn't already been the best Christmas Eve so far, the *Randall and Hopkirk (Deceased) Christmas Special* was just about to start.

Me, Maggie and Susan

Susan was in the same class as me and Maggie. She was dead brainy but she was skinny and ugly and Maggie, while a bit fat, was beautiful. Me, I wasn't brainy or beautiful, and I never would be so long as Mum kept perming my hair with the leftover perming lotion she kept under the sink after she'd done Auntie Annie's hair. All the good-looking boys fancied Maggie, the brainy ones fancied Susan and none of them fancied me. Whenever we got homework Susan would always get a gold star and me and Maggie, well, sometimes we got a star but it was never gold and mostly our pages were covered in red pen and Susan's, well, it was never covered in red pen, only stars, golden stars for the golden girl and after a while, that started to really get on my and Maggie's tits.

I was dead brilliant at Physical Education though. Maggie, she wasn't, 'cause she was fat, but she still came to the gym and put on her stretchy navy-blue school shorts and the boys circled around her like flies round shite, at least that's what Mum used to say. I could do the front splits without batting an eye, jump the high jump the highest, put the shot further than anybody ever had in the past and I was the only one, *ever*, to finish the egg-and-spoon race with the egg still on the spoon. I was brilliant at P.E. and nobody could take that away from me, not even Timothy Strachan, who, to be fair, could jump quite a distance in the long jump but nobody gave a fuck about him, 'cause he was poor and had to line up in the free-dinner queue at the school canteen. And even Susan, brainy fucking Susan, used to watch me in awe along with the rest of the class. I was the envy of my P.E. class and I loved it.

But nothing could take away the fact that Susan was the brainiest and each time she got her homework back from the teacher with another gold fucking star on it, she'd stare at that star on the page and her nostrils would flare in and out in self adoration.

So me and Maggie hatched a plan. The next day after P.E. we retreated to the changing room and pulled off our stretchy navy-blue shorts and black plimsolls. The whole school had to wear those black plimsolls with the stretchy panel in the front and Susan, well she was so fragile, so small, so *brainy*, she couldn't have the black school plimsolls like the rest of us. She had to have pretty pink slipperettes with the non-slip soles in case she hurt herself in the big nasty gymnasium. As if it wasn't bad enough she got special treatment in the classroom for being brainier than the rest of us, now she got special treatment in P.E. 'cause she was so fragile.

Maggie and I changed quickly out of our P.E. gear and into our school uniforms and our hearts were racing at the thought of our plan and the excitement made us shriek with laughter as we waited to get it underway. Eventually, Susan arrived, last back to the changing room as usual. Poor Susan, so fragile, so small, so brainy, that she had to take her time coming from the gymnasium lest she should hurt herself on the way. And as Susan busied herself getting out of her navy-blue stretchy shorts and pink slipperettes, Maggie and I pretended we weren't paying any attention to her at all and talked between ourselves about this and that, boys mostly, boys who fancied Maggie with her big tits and fat arse, and we racked our brains trying to come up with at least one boy who might fancy me in this lifetime, but none came to mind. And we watched Susan as she headed to the shower, then we made our move. We raced across to her open locker and there they were, those little pink fucking slipperettes with their non-slip soles and I looked at Maggie and Maggie looked at me.

'Right, grab them,' I said in a loud whisper.

'No, *you* grab them,' she loudly whispered back.

'No, *you* grab them. It was your fuckin' idea,' I said, the whisper no longer a whisper.

'No, *you* fuckin' grab them, we're in this together,' she almost shouted.

'Keep your voice down, for Chrissake. Right, let's both of us grab one each at the same time, that way I can't blame you and you can't blame me!' I whispered back.

So we did. We put our right hands into the locker and Maggie took one pink slipperette by the toe and I took the other pink slipperette by the heel and we ran together screaming like banshees down the corridor and crashed through the swing doors, nearly taking them off their hinges and out into the playground and we kept on running and screeching all the way to the other side of the school to the rubbish-bin compound and once we were there we stopped, each of us holding our pink slipperettes and laughing so hard that it hurt.

'Right, what now?' I panted.

'Let's throw them into that big bin there at the back, that way she'll *never* get them back,' Maggie said.

'Aye, good idea,' I said. 'Okay, I'll say one two three, then we'll throw them into the bin at the same time, then it's both our faults, right?' I said.

'Aye, right,' Maggie said, and just as we were about to count to three, Maggie looked at me and her eyes twinkled with badness. 'I've got an idea,' she said. 'Before we put them in the bin, why don't we rub them in that dog shite that's over there in the corner? That way, even if she does find them, she'll never want them back again with dog shite all over them.'

Quietly, I didn't think the dog shite was such a good

idea, but if I ever wanted to get a boyfriend I'd have to hang around with Maggie with her big tits and fat arse so I agreed with her and told her I thought it was a brilliant idea.

'Okay, let's do it,' I said and a strange sinking feeling settled in the pit of my stomach, the fun suddenly gone from it all. We made our way to that dog shite, each of us still holding our slipperettes, and we did what Maggie suggested. When we were done, we threw them into the big bin at the back and ran all the way back to the main school playground and neither of us was laughing anymore.

The plan that had seemed so much fun, so hilarious as we were hatching it, was no longer funny and I felt sick in my stomach. What harm had her slipperettes done us anyway? What harm did her braininess do us? It felt like a horrible mistake and when we saw her come out of the gym building carrying her little gym bag with tears in her eyes, I felt sick. She came up to us, 'cause we were her friends, and asked if we'd seen her slipperettes anywhere, that she'd lost them and if she went home without them her da would take the belt to her. I looked at her and wanted to cry with shame. So what if she was brainier than me? So what if her nostrils did flare in and out when she got her homework back from the teacher with another fucking gold star on it? So what if she was so fragile and her feet so small that she couldn't wear the black plimsolls like the rest of us?

Maggie thought the whole business was a hoot and she said later that if Susan's mother replaced the slipperettes then we should do the same next time we were in the gym. I laughed and told Maggie that was a brilliant idea but started to wonder if I was really that desperate to find a boyfriend. I was ashamed of myself and what I'd done and I vowed to myself right there and then that no matter how desperately I wanted a boyfriend, I'd never rub anybody else's pink slipperettes in dog shite again.

And Susan never found out what we'd done to her pink slipperettes and she went on getting the gold stars that made her nostrils flare and my best pal Maggie and me, well, we went on getting the red pen, and the terrible shame of the pink slipperettes would stay with us our whole lives long.

A few years later, just like I always knew she would, my best pal Maggie got herself a new best pal and her new best pal's name was Linda Hodgckiss. Linda had long, shiny chestnut hair and big tits too, just like Maggie, and one day in the playground they sang 'You are my Sunshine' and 'Nothing could be finer than to be in Carolina in the Morning' and that's when I went to the tuck shop and got myself a Curly Wurly.

I sat in the playground by myself at playtimes after that and I didn't care 'cause if I couldn't have Maggie as my best pal, then I didn't want anybody. And nobody asked me why Maggie wasn't my best pal anymore and why we weren't singing our songs together anymore and why we weren't going to each other's houses at lunchtime anymore. Nobody cared, 'cause Maggie and Linda just looked so right together, so shiny and chestnutty together, that everybody soon forgot that it was *me and Maggie* who played with the blue crayons that first day at school; that it was *me* who was Maggie's best pal first; that it was *me and Maggie* who sang 'You are my Sunshine' and 'Nothing could be finer than to be in Carolina in the Morning'; and that it was *me and Maggie* who were going to sing on a real stage one day and make so much money we'd have all the tinned macaroni and cheese that money could buy.

Buster's weekend by the sea

We had a caravan by the sea at Lendalfoot and my da used to let us go there sometimes with Mum on the weekends, so long as we'd collected all the milk money on the Friday night before. There was no sand there, just gravel and rocks and rock pools and crabs, and the waves would crash up hard against the rocks and if we were on the beach we'd have to run for cover. Mum bought us some fishing line once and we sat by the rock pools with our lines in the water forever and a day but we didn't catch anything and Mum said that didn't matter 'cause at least we were out getting the fresh air about our arses. The Irish Sea washed up dark-brown seaweed every day and if the sun came out the seaweed attracted millions of flies. Sometimes if we poked it with a stick a terrible smell would escape and we played a game of seeing who could run away from the smell the fastest.

We loved going to the caravan 'cause my da never came with us. It was brilliant. But even though he never came

Mum would be sad knowing he was up to no good with all those filthy whores at the pub while we were down by the sea getting the fresh air about our arses.

My da had bought our caravan cheap and we felt like royalty that first weekend we went there. Our caravan was number 15b and we made a rock garden at the front of it and planted nasturtiums and pansies that Mum had bought from the garden centre. There wasn't any electricity and when the sun went down we used to light up the gas mantles and sing songs and sometimes we'd go for long walks in the dark with Mum. We'd look across the sea to Paddy's Milestone where a solitary light flashed every night and we'd wonder who would be standing there with a torch like that flashing away and Mum told us it wasn't a torch but a lighthouse and its flashing light warned sailors not to come too close.

The caravan site had a shop where you could buy stuff like crisps and milk and Fairy Liquid and it was owned by Doogie who owned the caravan site. We used to call him, 'Doogie Woogie wi' the hairy nose' 'cause he had long hairs growing out of his nostrils and Mum said she wondered why Doogie's wife didn't just pluck the bloody hairs out or cut them off at least. One night after our dinner and once we'd sung all the songs we knew, we went to Doogie's shop and Mum bought us a packet of crisps each. I had pickled onion flavour 'cause they're my favourite and the four of us ran back to the caravan and huddled around the gas fire and ate them and Andrew invented a game. It was brilliant. You had to take your empty crisp bag and hold it up to the gas fire as close as you could get it and the heat from the fire would shrink the bag before your very eyes and whoever got their packet the smallest, so long as you could still read the writing, won the game. Andrew was the best at it 'cause he wasn't scared to burn his fingers, but I won the game once and you should have seen the size of the writing on my packet of pickled onion, it was tiny. That night Andrew got mad and said I was cheating, that his packet was the smallest, and Mum gave Andrew a crack on the arse and told him if he didn't sit down and behave himself then he could go outside and look at the flashing light on Paddy's Milestone for the rest of the night and we'd soon see how he liked that.

Once we took Buster with us to the caravan for the weekend and we had to be careful, 'cause Buster didn't like anybody else except us and we were always getting into trouble with the police at home 'cause he kept biting people who dared to come to our front door. We arrived at the caravan late that Friday night after we'd collected all the milk money in for my da. When we got up the next morning we took Buster to the sandy beach at the other end of the caravan park. The sandy beach was always deserted, except for this day, when there was another dog there. We knew this dog from the caravan park. Mum used to call him 'Auld Man McGuiness' and he was old and had a white beard and walked around minding his own business all day long. When Buster saw him that day he raced straight across the beach, grabbed Auld Man McGuiness by the throat, and shook him like a rag doll right there in front of us. When Buster finally released his grip Auld Man McGuiness lay dead in front of us and his white beard was stained red with his own blood. Me and Andrew just stood there screaming and Izzy, well, she ran up and grabbed Buster by his tartan collar and we all ran back to the caravan with Buster to tell Mum what had happened. When Mum heard she told us to get our belongings into the tartan holdall and fifteen minutes later we were in the car hightailing it out of town and Mum kept looking in her rear-view mirror for flashing blue lights.

When we got home my da wanted to know why we were back so early and Mum told him Buster had been bad and that this time he'd killed a dog on the beach and my da was that happy he sent Mum to the butcher to get Buster the biggest bone that money could buy. He even let Buster sit up on the couch that night. My da loved Buster and years later when Buster died of old age, my da had an oil painting done of him and hung it on the wall above his leather armchair in the good room.

We didn't go back to the caravan at Lendalfoot for a long, long time after that and when finally we did, it was winter and the nasturtiums and the pansies had all died for the want of a drink and Mum said she'd get new ones from the garden centre and we'd plant them next time we came down.

And none of us went to that sandy beach again for fear of seeing Auld Man McGuinness still lying there dead. So we played on the gravelly beach with its rock pools and crabs and as we played, the wind blew the rain horizontally and the Irish Sea washed up its dark-brown seaweed, though none of us had the mind for poking it with a stick and running away from the smell.

Rona fills her lungs at the caravan

My da came home one day and told us we were getting a new sister. And then he told us he was going to the children's home at Cathkin to pick up Rona and she was going to stay with us on the weekends from now on. He told us we'd better all be on our best behaviour and not be showing him up, else there'd be trouble. I asked my da why she was coming to stay with us and where was her own da and my da said I was to never fucking mind where her own da was, that her own da had put her in a children's home and that's why she was coming to spend time with us, in a normal family environment.

And so I asked my da what a normal family environment was when it was at home and that's when he told me, 'Less of your fuckin' cheek m'lady.' He told me to go and get my room tidied up and that he'd better not see me back out till it was done. And I walked off to my room and all the while I was thinking about this Rona and wondering who she thinks *she* is and why should we have to put up with somebody we don't even know just so *she* can spend time in a normal family environment. I tidied my room and by the time I'd finished my da had already left to go and get this Rona. I asked Mum what was going on and she said my da had taken it into his head to befriend a child from the children's home 'cause Jimmy at the pub was doing the same thing – as if we didn't have enough problems with my da's drinking and his womanising, now we had another mouth to feed.

So my da went to the children's home at Cathkin that day and brought back Rona. Rona had nine brothers and sisters and they were all in the home, too. She was twelve years old, one year older than me, and she had pale white skin and long black hair and she was skinny like a long drink of water, at least that's what Nanny used to say.

Rona arrived with a blue vinyl suitcase. My da told her she'd be sharing my bedroom and so I showed Rona my tidy bedroom and her side of the bed and then we all sat in the living room and had a cup of tea and a toasted soda scone from Joe Black's bakery on the Glasgow Road.

Mum made us a mince and onion curry that night for our tea and it was our way of making Rona feel special, 'cause it's not every day you get a mince and onion curry. When we finished eating I told Mum I hoped the electricity would get cut off again like that last time when we couldn't pay the bill so we could light the candles and show

Rona how to make a crocodile or maybe even a rabbit in the shadows on the wall. And that's when Mum kicked me under the table and told me to stop talking rubbish about electricity bills that couldn't be paid indeed.

The next day, my da said we should take Rona down to the caravan at Lendalfoot to get some sea air into her lungs. I asked Mum why he was so concerned with Rona's lungs when he'd never once mentioned my lungs before, and Mum said he must have been listening to Jimmy at the pub again. So we packed up the tartan holdall and headed off to the caravan like he said. Me and Andrew sat in the back of the car on either side of Rona, and Izzy sat in the front with Mum, Once we were on the road Andrew started to sing that song I had made up for the school competition that time, trying to embarrass me in front of Rona, and I told him if he didn't shut up I was going to kill him when I got to the caravan and he just kept on singing. Then he said, 'Why wait till you get to the caravan? Why don't you kill me right now?' And so I leaned across Rona and tried to batter him in the face and Mum shouted from the front to bloody well behave ourselves or she'd turn the car around and we'd head back home. So I sat back in my seat and gave Andrew a look and he knew he was getting it when we got to the caravan.

I ignored Andrew for the rest of the journey after that and spoke to Rona in a quiet voice so that Andrew couldn't hear me. I told Rona about the rocky beach at the caravan and the seaweed that gets washed in all the way from Ireland and how it stinks in the summer if you poke it with a stick. And I told her about the flashing light on Paddy's Milestone and the green hills dotted with sheep and Auld Snib, the local tramp who used to eat dead seagulls, and then I told her about Sawney Bean, the cannibal who ate a thousand people in his lifetime and who lived in a cave not far from where our own caravan stood. And I told Rona about Doogie Woogie with the hairy nose and the crisp packets we would shrink in front of the gas fire and the chicken noodle soup Mum would make us out of the packet when the sun went down that night.

Once we got to the caravan Rona's eyes were wide with excitement and she didn't know which way to turn first. While Izzy and Andrew helped Mum to unload the car, me and Rona pulled off our socks and shoes and raced to the beach and the two of us ran barefoot across the rocks like we'd known each other forever and our lungs were filled with the salty sea air. As we ran I could see Rona's long black hair flapping in the wind in front of me and when she turned around her cheeks were pink and her eyes were sparkling, and that's when I knew what Jimmy at the pub had meant about getting the sea air into her lungs. As we scrambled over the rocks we came across a rock pool and I lifted a rock to show Rona where the crabs sometimes hide and just then a tiny crab raced out sideways. I picked it up to show Rona and the tiny crab scurried up and down my thumb and I wasn't scared one bit. Then Rona bent down and pulled a shell off the side of the rock and she told me the creature inside was called a whelk. Then she told me she had seen them in a jar in Vladimir's deli at the Gorbals once, the same deli Mum used to buy our pork ring sausages from, and that people eat those whelks with a pin, and I said that was disgusting, that I'd never eat a whelk no matter how hungry I was, and Rona said she'd never eat one either. When we'd finished with the whelks and the crabs, the wind started to blow in all the way from Ireland and we huddled up close together against the rocks and looked across the deserted beach. We gave a name to our deserted beach that day and we called it Al-Ron Bay, our secret code for Ali and Rona Bay.

Rona came to our house every weekend after that and once she brought her youngest sister Diane and another time she brought her sister Jo, and once she even brought her brother Stewart. As Rona became a part of our family she taught us stuff we never knew – and I don't mean how to pull whelks off the rocks and how to eat them from the jar with a pin if you've a mind to. She taught us that we were lucky to have a mammy who made us chicken noodle soup out of the packet when the sun went down at night, and that my da, although he spent every minute of every day making our lives miserable, at least hadn't put us in a children's home where there's no mammy to make you feel safe and all you've got to look forward to are strangers coming on the weekend to show you what a normal family environment is like.

On Sunday nights we'd take Rona back to the children's home where she shared a room with twenty others and we'd say goodbye to her at the door and tell her we'd see her the following Friday. And then we'd get back into the car and Rona would stand at the door by herself and wave until we'd disappeared out of sight, and we'd ask Mum why Rona couldn't just stay with us all the time and Mum said it wasn't that simple, 'cause some day Rona's real mammy might show up to take Rona back again and Rona had to be there in case she did. But Rona's real mammy wasn't able to take her back and years later, when Rona was old enough, the day came for her to leave the children's home. She packed her blue vinyl suitcase and took the bus to our place to say goodbye 'cause she was leaving Scotland for good to go and live in England. We asked her what was wrong with Scotland and she said there was nothing wrong with Scotland, just that she needed to get as far away from the ghosts of her past as she could and we could understand that, I mean, who couldn't?

So we hugged and said goodbye to Rona and our hearts were heavy 'cause we didn't want to imagine our lives without her. And as we shared our last few moments together she took my hand, 'cause we were sisters, and she told me she would miss me and I said I would miss her, too. Then she kissed me on the forehead and she told me all we had to do was think of Al-Ron Bay and we'd always be together. I tried to smile instead of crying and when I looked at her through my watery eyes, I saw that her cheeks were pink and her eyes were sparkling and I watched her as she walked away towards her new life in England and her black hair flapped in the wind and I never saw her again.

Dandy the pony and the blue rosette

Our cousin David lived on the other side of our town and his da was called Jack. Jack was our da's brother so that made him our Uncle Jack. Uncle Jack was married to Georgina and they had stables on their land and a fat white pony called Dandy and a tall shiny chestnut horse called Sorrito. David used to ride Sorrito at the local gymkhana and sometimes he won blue rosettes with 'First' on them. He used to stick them on his bedroom wall, right next to his bed, and when he went to his bed at night the moon would come in through the window and shine on his blue rosettes and David would fall asleep contented. And one day I told David I wished I had a pony so I could get blue rosettes at the local gymkhana and he said, 'How can you get the blue rosettes if I'm gettin' them?'

Sometimes after school I would go to David's place and we would go out riding together and David always rode Sorrito and I was only ever allowed to ride Dandy.

When we went riding David wore beige stretchy trousers with patches on the inside thighs that went right down to his knees and a proper velvet riding hat and I used to wear my polyester trewsers that chafed the inside of my thighs and the crash helmet that my Uncle Bruce got me that time he worked on the building site in Spain.

One day after school, David and I saddled up Dandy and Sorrito and we trotted out of the stables and on to Bardykes Road that would lead us to the fields where we'd ride like the wind. The air was icy cold that day and a thick frost covered the road and as I sat in the saddle I watched the warm steam rise from Dandy's nostrils and the sparks as they flew from Sorrito's hooves as she tried to grip the icy road in front of me. I called out to David to tell him about the sparks and David turned around and called out above Sorrito's snorting and tail swishing that her hooves were sparking 'cause she was getting ready to fly, that she was a flying machine and she could fly him anywhere in the world he wanted to go. And that's when I thought back to Maggie when she was still my best pal and how she told me she had a golden eagle that used to visit her all the way from Africa. Her golden eagle would come to her house in the middle of the night and pick her up in its wings and take her all over the world and then it would bring her back home again and drop her back in the safety of her own bed. After that her golden eagle would disappear into thin air and Maggie told me she was never sad 'cause she knew that her golden eagle would always come back. And years later, when Maggie's mum died, Maggie said her golden eagle came and took her mum to Africa, to Madagascar in fact, and Maggie said her mum was happier there than she'd ever been in her hometown where all she'd had to look forward to was Friday nights at the bingo and the occasional Bacardi and Coke at the Miners' Welfare Club.

David and I trotted along the last stretch of frosty road and as we neared the open fields, David guided Sorrito into a gentle canter and my little fat Dandy followed suit. Before I knew it, David and I were cantering through green field after green field and the rhythm was comforting and my crash helmet from the building site in Spain fell from my head and bounced along in the grass behind me and I didn't care. With the wind in my hair I stood up in my stirrups and breathed in the freedom and I didn't want it to end. Just then a big black bat flew out from an old oak tree and gave Dandy such a fright he reared up on his back legs, just like Black Beauty did on the telly on a Tuesday night, and I started to slide backwards out of my saddle. But I held on tight to Dandy's neck and next thing I knew Dandy was jumping forward onto his front legs and that's when I felt my feet lose their grip in the stirrups and I left the saddle and flew through the air and landed on my chin on the only rock to be found right there in the green grassy fields.

I seemed to lie on the ground for a long, long time and when I stood up I touched my face and blood leaked from the gash the rock had made under my chin, staining my T-shirt and the green grass bright red. Once David realised I wasn't cantering behind him he came galloping back and Dandy reared up on his back legs again and David jumped off Sorrito's back and quickly took Dandy by the reins and told him, 'Whoa boy! Whoa boy!' like you hear sometimes on those cowboy movies you get on telly on a Saturday afternoon. David told me he won a blue rosette once for something called horsemanship and that he knew exactly what to do to make Dandy calm again and he stroked that part of Dandy's head between his eyes that ponies love to have stroked. All the while he whispered into Dandy's ear that he was a good boy and eventually Dandy did calm down and the fast steam coming out of his nostrils slowed until finally Dandy was still and calm and not wanting to do his Tuesday night Black Beauty impressions any more.

With Dandy calm David turned to look at me and when he saw the blood streaming down my throat and saturating my T-shirt, he looked like he'd seen a ghost. He told me to stay where I was and to hold Dandy's reins, that he was going back home to get some help, and then he jumped onto Sorrito's back and took off into the sunset just like in those movies again. I stayed behind with Dandy and the bats and the soft orange glow from the sun as it disappeared down behind the green grassy fields.

The darkness came quickly and I kept on stroking Dandy in that bit between his eyes that ponies love to have stroked and I listened to the owls make that '*too-wit too-woo*' sound you hear in scary movies sometimes. Then, for a moment, I stopped stroking Dandy and turned to see the owls, and I stared at the moon and I thought about David's blue rosettes on his bedroom wall. I watched the bats as they came and went from their old oak tree until Dandy nudged me in the waist and nearly knocked me off my feet. He put his head down by my hand as if to say, stroke me again, right there in that bit between my eyes, and I smiled and cuddled him and my bloodied T-shirt left a red stain on his soft white coat. Then I told him he was a naughty boy and I said, 'Whoa boy!' a few times just to see what it felt like and it felt stupid standing there in the dark talking like a cowboy from one of those movies on a Saturday afternoon and I was glad there was nobody around to hear me.

Twenty minutes later, I saw the headlights of a car approaching and as it got nearer I could see it was David and his mum, Georgina, in their green Volvo estate. Georgina got out of the car first and she took one look at me and said, 'Hospital for you m'lady,' 'cause I might have something called concussion and then she said I might even need to get some stitches in my chin by the look of that cut. When I thought about the stitches, secretly I was pleased, 'cause I knew I wouldn't have to go to school the next day and I'd probably get to eat biscuits in bed that night.

When we got to the hospital the doctor asked me how many fingers he was holding up and if I felt dizzy and I told him three fingers and that I didn't feel dizzy at all, although secretly I wished I did. He said I was going to be okay but he'd have to put a few stitches in my chin and give me an injection in the bum for something called lock-jaw. He got the needle out and I was brave like a soldier and didn't cry, and when he finished I tried to glimpse my reflection in the mirror above the sink to see how sore the stitches looked. When I limped out of the doctor's room David and Georgina were waiting for me and Georgina gave me a cuddle and told me not to worry, that Mum was on her way.

While we waited for Mum to arrive, Georgina bought me and David a Fry's Chocolate Cream each from the chocolate machine in the waiting room, and David said I'd handled myself like a true horsewoman out there in the fields that day. He said if I handled myself like that at the gymkhana one day then I'd win a blue rosette for sure. And then Georgina told him he should give me the present now and that's when David came up to me and shook my hand like they do at the gymkhana when you win a prize and he handed me my first blue rosette. In the middle it said 'First' and underneath it said 'Horsemanship'.

When I got home from the hospital I stuck my blue rosette to my bedroom wall and that night when I went to bed with my packet of biscuits, the moonlight came in through the bedroom window and shone on my blue rosette and I fell asleep contented.

The day my da took our ponies to the glue factory

Even though I had a scar from the time Dandy threw me from the saddle, I desperately wanted a pony of my own. One day I asked Mum if I could and she said we'd hardly enough money to feed ourselves never mind a bloody pony. That same week my Uncle Jack told my da his pal Hughie had two flea-bitten ponies he wanted to get rid of and so my da said he would take them. He went to Hughie's place with Uncle Jack that very day and they put the ponies into Uncle Jack's horsebox and the two of them brought the ponies home. One of the ponies was a rusty colour and the other was silver and so we called them Rusty and Silver. Mum made a bed for them that night in the greenhouses on the land at the back of our house with the four bales of straw that Hughie had sent and Rusty and Silver had to share those greenhouses with Annie the donkey and Ducky and Drakey, the duck and drake who mysteriously appeared in our driveway one Sunday afternoon and decided to stay.

Me and Izzy and Andrew cleaned out Rusty and Silver's greenhouse every morning and brushed them every night with the wire brush Mum kept under the sink and they ran around happily all day long on our big block of land. We picked fresh grass and chicken weed for them every day from the field across the road and sometimes we wished we could get hay for them, but my da said there was no way he was spending good money on hay for those useless fucking animals, so they ate what they got and they didn't seem to mind at all.

Some nights after we said goodnight to the ponies, Mum struggled to breathe. And one night when she could hardly breathe at all my da had to phone the doctor. While we waited for the doctor to come I looked at Mum wrapped in a blanket and sitting on the orange vinyl swivel chair she'd got at Big Marion's and she didn't look well. Even though the doctor was on his way I was still worried and I told myself over and over that things would be okay. When the doctor finally arrived my da told me I should get out of the room to give Mum peace so I moved outside into the hallway and peered through the dimpled-glass door and I looked at a hundred reflections of her and begged God to not let her die. I watched the doctor as he brought out his stethoscope and listened to Mum's chest and lungs and I feared the worst when he shook his head and announced it was no good. The doctor said she had to go to the hospital and before I knew what was happening the ambulance had arrived and Mum was wrapped up in another blanket and carted out of the house. I stood behind the safety of my dimpled-glass door and watched a hundred blue lights flash their way into the distance, until I couldn't see anything anymore, and then I stared back at the empty orange swivel chair where Mum had sat just a moment before and I bit my lip and promised myself I wouldn't cry. 'Behave yersel!' That's what Mum used to say when she saw we were about to cry. And I tried to behave myself right there and then, but it was no good and the tears leaked from the corners of my eyes.

When Nanny got the news that Mum was in the hospital she raced to our place to make sure we'd get fed while Mum was gone. She arrived wearing her knitted beanie and Grampa's leather slippers and she'd run all the way from 9 Maitland Avenue, pulling her two-wheeled tartan shopping trolley behind her.

'Awright, Nannie!' Andrew called out, excited to see her as he always was.

'Awright, son. Come on, gie yir Nanny a wee hand with the trolley now.' Andrew raced over and lifted the top of the trolley and looked inside.

'Any goodies for us, Nanny?' Andrew asked.

'There's nae goodies in there for you today, just some dinner. When I heard about your mum, I just ran and ran to get here. I woulda got a lift but your Uncle Bruce is still in the Swiss Alps skiing with Father Frances.' And Nanny paused for breath and looked down at her feet in surprise and went on, 'Just look at me, will you, I'm still wearing yer Grampa's slippers.'

'You always wear Grampa's slippers, Nanny,' I said.

'Aye, true enough. Right, let's get the tea on,' she said and made her way to the kitchen.

Nanny had brought a pound of mince and a three-pound bag of Maris Piper potatoes and she got the pots onto the gas stove straightaway. When the dinner was ready she called us to come to the kitchen and pick up our plates and then we took them to the living room and sat on the couch with our plates on our knees. I didn't like the look of the colour of nanny's mince and the first mouthful confirmed the worst. It tasted like shite. Of course I didn't want to upset Nanny and so I said nothing and just played with it for a while, pushing the morsels of mince this way and that around the plate and mixing it in with the potatoes, all the while looking around the room for somewhere to hide it.

Goldie, our goldfish, was swimming around in his tank on top of Mum's walnut sideboard enjoying himself in his nice clean tank, and so I picked up my plate and moved across to the sideboard and had a chat to Goldie, all the while still pushing the morsels of mince and mashed tatties around my plate. And as we chatted I kept one eye on Goldie and the other on Nanny who was busying herself in the kitchen with this and that and when she wasn't looking, I took huge forkfuls of that mince and tatties and shovelled them into Goldie's tank, and I kept on shovelling and shovelling until nothing on my plate remained. And then, when there was nothing left to shovel, I held the plate above the tank and scraped in the gravy with my fork. When it was all gone I placed my cutlery on my empty plate and sat back in my chair relieved.

Of course, I thought the mince and tatties would just land at the bottom of the tank in amongst the gravel and nobody would be any the wiser and then when Mum got out of hospital she could just clean out the tank like she always did. But when I looked into the tank I saw that Goldie's once-clear tank was now a gravy-filled swamp and through the swamp I could see Goldie trying to swim, his little fins flapping furiously. His tank had become a quagmire and no matter how hard he tried Goldie couldn't move. I pressed my nose on the side of the cold tank and looked at him in horror and he looked back at me, in pain and unable to breathe. But he knew I hadn't meant to hurt him and he knew that I loved him and looking into his closing eyes, I knew that he loved me, too. As he hovered in the gravy with no energy left, Goldie gave up the fight to live and flipped himself onto his side and floated to the top of his once-clear tank.

Weeping for Goldie and my stupidity I got a tartan tea-towel out from the tea-towel drawer and placed it over his tank as a mark of respect and decided if anybody asked me what had happened I would cry and hold my breath till my face went blue, 'cause when I did that nobody bothered me with questions I didn't want to answer.

When we went to visit Mum at the hospital the next day they had hooked her up to a machine and put a mask on her face so she could breathe the oxygen from the big tanks at the side of her bed. We made her get-well-soon cards and Andrew made the best one. It was huge and he drew roses on the front with the big red crayon he stole from Mrs MacAlpine's desk at school. On the front of the card he wrote: *Dear Mum I love you 'cause you are like a rose*, and inside he wrote, *and you have a smile too.* Mum cried when she read that card and she folded it and kept it in her handbag for the next seventeen years.

We drew pictures of the animals for Mum and we told her that the animals missed her just like we did. We wanted to take them to the hospital with us and hold them up at the window next to Mum's bed so she could wave to them, but my da said no. So the animals stayed behind and they, too, counted the days until Mum came back.

The doctors said Mum had had an asthma attack and it was brought on by an allergy to our ponies, so not long after Mum got out of hospital my da told us he was taking Rusty and Silver to the glue factory after all the trouble they'd caused. As if it wasn't bad enough that Goldie the goldfish died when Mum got sick, now Rusty and Silver were going to die too.

And so the day came when we had to say goodbye to them. Me and Mum and Izzy and Andrew went down to the greenhouse that morning and fed them the grass and the chicken weed we'd picked for them from the field across the road, and I put my arms around Rusty's big head and stroked his mane and he nudged his nose into my side and nearly knocked me off my feet and I laughed and held his big head closer. Silver watched on from the other side of the greenhouse and when she saw Rusty getting all the attention she raced across and nudged her nose into my other side and swished her tail and snorted through those big nostrils of hers.

And I held their big heads in my arms and kissed them both on the soft skin of their noses and they looked at me with their big brown eyes as if to say, Don't forget about us.

And I whispered into both their ears, 'As if I could.'

The houses that Bruce built

Many years after Chick died, Nanny and Grampa and Bruce still lived together in their council house at 9 Maitland Avenue. Their house was close to the graveyard where Chick was buried and every Sunday we went to the graveyard and put flowers on Chick's grave and sometimes Grampa planted white snowdrops and blue forget-me-nots around the headstone.

Bruce was still working as a builder though not always in Spain. Once he even worked on a building site as far away as Australia and he lived in a house right next door to the beach. But Bruce never went to the beach 'cause he preferred the cold and the snow like you get in Scotland, where icy winds bite you and turn your pale cheeks red and how could the beach ever compete with the likes of that, when all it offers you is sand in your trunks and sea salt in your hair and the promise of a good scorching from the midday sun that leaves you wanting to die? So Bruce built what needed to be built in Australia and then he left that place for good and went back to Scotland where the icy wind bit him and he knew he was alive.

One day Bruce and my da decided what a great idea it would be to build two semi-detached bungalows on the two-and-a-half acres of land behind our little house, so we could all live next door to each other in harmony in our red-brick Seventies bungalows, just like one big happy family and everybody agreed. Nanny, Grampa and Bruce would live in one of the bungalows and we would live in the other. The bungalows took a long time to build 'cause we could only buy bricks and cement whenever we had the money. Bruce spent more time away from Scotland skiing in the Swiss Alps than he should have, but when he wasn't skiing he worked hard on getting the bungalows built and all of us helped and finally, with lots of shouting and unreasonable demands, the bungalows got finished, albeit five years later.

Me and Izzy and Andrew worked on the bungalows every day with Bruce after we'd done our homework. I didn't like doing my homework but Mum promised if I did it every night from then until the following year when I went to the high school, she'd tell Bruce to build an extra space in my bedroom to put a desk and a desk lamp, and when Mum told me that, I promised I would do my homework every night in the week.

Building those bungalows was hard work but it was

exciting and brilliant. Our favourite bit was when Bruce would call a tea break and we'd all sit down to pork ring sausages (that everybody ate except me) and jars of pickled gherkins and sour-dough bread sandwiches. We felt like real labourers who had earned their tea and we ate our sandwiches with filthy hands, and Bruce always finished his tea break with a cigarette and he drew long and hard on it and said nothing for fear it would spoil the pleasure of the nicotine entering his blood. Sometimes when we looked at him it seemed that his cigarette transported him to another world, maybe the world of Lederhosen and après-ski on the piste, and he looked like he savoured those moments alone with his cigarette more than he savoured life itself.

Bruce was a professional builder and he knew everything. That meant that he had to have an assistant every day and if you were chosen to be his assistant for the day you had to spend that day carrying bricks up and down ladders, sweeping up Bruce's mess and putting the kettle on to make his coffee. Bruce took seven sugars in his coffee and sometimes he would say, 'Put the seven sugars in the cup and don't stir it – I don't like it too sweet,' and we would laugh and think he was mad.

Bruce and my da shared the costs of the bricks and cement and all the other ingredients we needed to build the bungalows and as we built, we dreamed of what it would be like to live in our semi-detached three-bedroom bungalows, with our fitted kitchens and avocado bathroom suites. Even before the walls were built we all knew where our bedrooms were going to be and if I saw Andrew walk across the foundations of my room, I'd tell him, 'Get out of my fuckin' room right now!' and he'd run and hide and Bruce would laugh and light a cigarette and tell me to put the kettle on. It was going to be a dream come true to live there, all of us together, and all of us were excited.

Finally, the long and arduous task of building the bungalows came to an end and all that was left to do was paint the woodwork with shiny gloss paint and of course it was up to Mum to do the painting 'cause my da, he couldn't even change a light bulb never mind paint a room. Every time Mum finished a room Quackers, our one-eyed cat, would come in and rub himself against the sticky skirting boards and one-eyed or not, Mum would curse him and chase him from the room. Once she had picked every cat hair from every skirting board in the house, we moved ourselves in.

The first few years of living next door to each other passed peacefully and Bruce painted his living-room walls lilac and we laughed at him and Mum said we shouldn't laugh, 'cause Bruce painted his living-room walls lilac 'cause he was artistic and that made us laugh all the more.

Nanny used to come and go happily between the houses, from her own back door straight to our back door and into our kitchen, where me, Izzy, Andrew and Mum spent most of our time. My da spent most of his time in the good room by himself sitting on his leather armchair by the side of the gas fire, with his oil painting of Buster hanging right above his head. When Nanny came to visit she always had goodies for us from the market and it was brilliant. She was the kindest and most generous woman I've ever known and Mum takes after her in every way, except Mum doesn't wear a beanie and Grampa's leather slippers. Nanny would bring everything via those backdoors from pork ring sausages to leather-soled Italian shoes that had only been worn once, if you don't mind, and every day she came was like Christmas Day, the kind of Christmas days we'd dream about where my da would be somewhere else, preferably dead.

Then the joy of living in close proximity to those we loved suddenly stopped and it stopped on precisely the day that Bruce asked my da for the title deeds to his own semi-detached bungalow, the semi-detached bungalow Bruce had built with his own hands and paid for with his own money, the semi-detached bungalow that Nanny and Grampa were to live out the rest of their lives in.

And my da told Bruce he couldn't have those deeds. He said no because Bruce's semi-detached bungalow was sitting on *my da's* two-and-a-half acres of land and according to my da that meant Bruce's semi-detached bungalow really belonged to him and if Bruce wanted the title deeds then he was going to have to take my da to court to get them.

And of course Bruce was never going to take his sister's husband to court and he hoped instead that he could appeal to my da's reason. But my da's a stranger to reason so all attempts at trying to resolve the matter between them failed and in the end relations broke down and my da stopped talking to Bruce and Nanny and Grampa. That's when my da decided he wanted fucking rid of them from the bungalow next door and he started on a campaign to make their lives unbearable so they'd end up desperate to move and my da would get to keep both properties for himself.

With my da now refusing to speak directly with Bruce he made me the messenger of his unreasonable demands and offensive orders and whenever he wanted to get a message to Bruce about him vacating the property my da would send me next door with strict instructions on what to tell 'that bastard Bruce'. Sometimes when I went next door to deliver those messages I'd find Bruce in front of the fire eating a huge plate of spaghetti Bolognese that Nanny had made him. He would give me a fork and I'd sit down in front of the fire too and share that big plate of spaghetti with him. One night he showed me how to twist the spaghetti using just my fork and he gave me a glass of red wine with a spoonful of sugar in it and we sat there slurping and sucking up strands of spaghetti together until eventually I'd forgotten what I had gone in there for. But once the spaghetti was finished I remembered again and so I'd give Bruce the message from my da and then I'd leave Bruce's place ashamed and go back next door and give my da Bruce's answer, which was always that he wasn't going anywhere until he got the title deeds to his house. And my da would get right fucking mad and start shouting like a loony and banging on the walls so loud that Bruce and Nanny and Grampa had no choice but to hear.

After some time I was too ashamed to deliver the messages from my da so whenever he sent me next door again to give a message to that bastard Bruce, I'd just go and see Bruce and have some spaghetti and a glass of red wine with a spoonful of sugar in it and we'd sit in front of the fire and I'd tell Bruce nothing and instead I'd listen to him tell me tales about skiing down icy slopes and through snowy pine forests in Switzerland. Then when the spaghetti and the stories were over I'd go back home with no reply to my da's message and then the screaming and shouting would start again.

Bruce stayed put with Nanny and Grampa as long as he could and my da's shouting and screaming made life unbearable for them. One day my da's pal, Peter the undertaker, needed to park his hearse somewhere for a few days and my da said it would be okay to park it on our two-and-a-half acres and he told Peter to park it right outside Nanny and Grampa's lounge-room window. And Nanny and Grampa had to look at that car night and day and their hearts were heavier than before and they wondered if they'd ever see an end to the pain and trauma of living in close proximity to those they loved with their fitted kitchens and avocado bathroom suites.

Throughout all the unrest Nanny still came to visit us via the back doors and sometimes when she arrived she'd run into my da in the kitchen and she didn't know what to say. But it didn't stop her coming and still she brought goodies for all of us including woollen socks for my da's sensitive feet, the only sensitive part about him, and her kindness and generosity never faltered during the most stressful time of her life, when she was nearly 80 years old and should have been living in peace in close proximity to those she loved. This was the time in Nanny's life when we should have been listening to her tell stories about her life around the table in front of the open fire eating spaghetti Bolognese and drinking red wine with a spoonful of sugar in it. Instead, all of us lived in fear and dreamed of how life could have been and my da continued to shout and scream and Nanny and Grampa sat together next door in their lilac living room with heavy hearts and stared out of their window into the waiting hearse.

My new best pal

Mum said I shouldn't worry about starting high school with no best pals to hang about with on my first day, but it's hard when you're standing there in the playground wishing there was somebody you could talk to, and then you start raking in your bag pretending you're trying to find something and there's only so many times you can do that before people start to notice and think there's something wrong with you. Mum said making good pals is something that takes time but then I thought, well, me and Maggie didn't take any time at all 'cause we were best pals on that first day we met at school.

So I just sat in the playground at break times on my own and tried to look like I didn't care. Mum had given me another home perm and my hair had gone yellow again and everybody sniggered at me in the corridor as I walked past them between classes. And sometimes I'd hide in the toilets at break time so that nobody could see me and

I'd pass the time thinking about my old best pal Maggie and how she never used to laugh at any of my perms and the more I thought about Maggie, the more I missed her and the more I missed her, the more I knew I'd never get another best pal just like her.

When I was in the playground I'd watch the groups of girls all huddled together in their own private circles and I wished I could have huddled in their private circles too, but nobody asked me. And sometimes I'd go to the tuck shop to give myself something to do and I'd get myself a Cadbury's Creme Egg and peel off the shiny paper from around it and I'd bite the top off and then I'd lick out the creamy stuff inside like they do on the telly and then when I was finished, I'd pick the skin from around my fingernails till they bled and wait for the next class to start.

Then, one day, Morag Black came up to me in the playground and she said I was only hanging around by myself 'cause I thought I was too good for everybody there. And how could I tell her that that wasn't true, that I wanted to be in one of their private circles hanging around in the playground talking about boys and lipstick and God alone knows what. Then she put me up against the wall and told me I was a fucking snob and that I was lucky she didn't kick my fucking arse and take my dinner money off me and when she let me go I ran straight to the toilets and locked myself in a cubicle and thought about my old best pal Maggie again.

As if it wasn't bad enough that nobody wanted to know me in the playground, the teachers in the English department didn't want to know me either 'cause I kept failing their stupid exams. One day Miss Clarke the English teacher asked me what it was about interpreting the works of the great writers and poets of our time that I didn't get. And that's when I told her I wished we could just read the great writers and poets of our time and enjoy them without having to pull them apart and answer questions on what they were thinking about at the time they wrote the stuff and she didn't seem to like that answer very much. And then she said if I wanted to keep on studying English I had to try harder, and while she was at it she said as if my interpretation skills weren't bad enough my handwriting was shite too, and that she'd never seen handwriting as bad as mine in her entire life and that was saying something 'cause her da was a doctor. And I told her my da's no' a doctor and his handwriting's shite too and that's when she told me one more word like that from you my lady and you'll find yourself outside the headmaster's door.

And so I thought I was trying harder but still I kept failing the exams and on the last exam I failed Miss Clarke wrote at the bottom of the page in red ink, 'Ask your mother to contact the English department in the first instance.' I didn't know what 'the first instance' meant but Mum seemed to know.

So Mum went up to the school the next day and knocked on the door of the English department and Miss Clarke opened the door and told Mum to come in and sit down and she went to the filing cabinet and brought out copies of my past exam papers and showed them to Mum. Mum looked through the papers with the red crosses, and then she looked up at Miss Clarke and said, 'So what's the problem?' And Miss Clarke said the problem was that I didn't have a clue about what was required of me to complete the English course and that they were going to have to give my place to another child with more ability who wouldn't drag down the morale of the brighter students. Mum asked Miss Clarke what I would do in place of English and Miss Clarke said there were still some places left in the chemistry class and then Mum said, do you think if Ali can't understand a poem, she'll be able to understand what's going on in chemistry? And that's when Miss Clarke stood up and said that wasn't her problem, and closed my file and stamped something on the front with a big rubber stamp and showed Mum the door.

When Mum came home that night she told me I couldn't take the English class anymore 'cause they had to give my place to another child with more ability. And then I said to Mum, 'First it was long division I couldn't do in the arithmetic class and now it's English. What's left, Mum? What am I good at?' And Mum said I was good at plenty of things.

'Like what?'

'Well, I mean, there's ... oh, I mean, let me think ... there must be a hundred things you're good at.'

And I said, 'Name one, Mum,' and she said, 'Well, needlework. There. You're good at needlework.'

'I am not, Mum. I'm shite at needlework. You saw that skirt I tried to make that time and even you said it was shite.'

'Aye, well, that's true. Now, look, I know, you're good at P.E! See, I told you you were good at something!'

'You did not, Mum, you told me I was good at *plenty* of things – P.E's only *one* thing.'

And so I ended up in chemistry. Nobody asked me if I even wanted to join that class and next thing I know, I'm having to show up at Room E11 in the Science Block on Monday mornings at ten o'clock for an hour of drudgery and it may as well have been in Chinese for all I understood. I sat by myself 'cause nobody wanted to know me in the chemistry class either and I made friends with the Bunsen burners and the test tubes and the things to stand the test tubes in. I hated chemistry and while Mrs Berry the chemistry teacher was going on about electrons and neutrons and hydrogen and carbon, my mind turned to Maggie in the English class probably writing poems and stories and reading Macbeth aloud in front of the class with her new best pal Linda with the shiny chestnut hair and the big tits while I sat in Room E11 with the Bunsen burners and the test tubes and the things to stand the test tubes in, writing out lines of x's and y's and talking about the periodic table of elements and who gives a fuck.

Then one Monday morning as I sat at my desk waiting for Mrs Berry to explain the difference between single bonds and double bonds somebody came and sat beside me. She took her books out of her bag and turned to me and smiled and said hello and I couldn't believe it and so I smiled and said hello back. She told me her name was Leanne and she offered me one of her sweeties and I told her you weren't allowed to eat sweeties in the class and that's when she said 'Who gives a fuck?' and so I smiled and took a sweetie from her and I hid it under my tongue and the two of us smiled some more.

A fine Johnny

Leanne was a brilliant new best pal. She had long golden hair and legs like two sticks of dry spaghetti that poked out of short pink skirts and the boys buzzed around Leanne just like they'd buzzed around Maggie, like flies 'round shite, at least that's what Mum used to say. And just like before, the boys never buzzed around me, and when they started to gather around Leanne I'd walk away to leave them alone together and nobody even noticed I wasn't there.

When four o'clock came I'd take a short cut home from school across the grass you weren't meant to walk on and I'd squeeze myself through the railings of the fence that led onto Camper Street. Brian Stewart's da's pet shop was just across from the railings on Camper Street and as I passed I'd look in the window at the black fan-tailed fish with the googly eyes. Mr Stewart would be standing behind his counter and he'd smile through the window and mouth a big 'hello!' to me and I'd smile back and mouth a big 'hello!' to him, and we did that every afternoon at four o'clock.

I'd wanted to go into the pet shop that day and tell Mr Stewart about the article I'd read in *Fish Weekly* about what to do when your fantail's under the weather and how you should feed it a frozen pea, defrosted, when out of nowhere this good-looking boy appeared and asked if he could carry my bag. I didn't know where to look, so I stared at my shoes and said, 'Aye, if you like.' He said he did like and gently took my bag and slung it over his shoulder on top of his own. He told me his name was Johnny, and what a fine Johnny he was too, and I let him carry my bag all the way to my street, though not to my house, for who wants to be caught by their da standing in the street with a boy in broad daylight. I took my bag from him and thanked him very much and all the while my face was purple with the embarrassment of it all like the beetroots Mum got at the markets and sometimes boiled whole. He asked me if he could carry my bag again the next day at four o'clock and I said, Aye all right, if you like, and he said he did like and I felt so happy I thought my heart would explode.

The phone was ringing when I walked into the house and I raced to answer it. It was Laughlin from the building site my da was working on. I put my hand over the mouthpiece and I shouted to Mum that Laughlin was on the phone and he needed to speak to her.

'Hello, Laughlin, it's Betty here,' Mum said, bending down and holding the phone away from her ear so's I could listen in.

'Aye, hello, Betty,' Laughlin said, ' I'm sorry to trouble you, hen, but it's about your man, big Joe.'

'Aye, go on,' Mum said.

'Well, I'm afraid it's bad news, Betty. There's been a terrible accident,'

'What do you mean, *terrible* accident? How terrible are we talking here?' Mum asked and I watched her eyes widen and a smile appear on the corners of her lips.

'Well, I don't want you to go worrying yourself half to death, but it's terrible enough.'

'Go on,' Mum said.

'Well, hen, big Gavyn, the crane driver, was working the crane, moving railway sleepers from one pile to another. Anyway, he only went and took his eyes off the job for a split second to unwrap his sandwiches when he accidentally knocked the button that released the brake and the railway sleeper went hurtlin' through the air and landed slap bang on big Joe's leg!'

'You don't say! So what kind of state's Joe in? Will he live?'

'Och aye, hen. I mean, don't get me wrong, it was a close call, but it's just his thigh bone that's broken and believe it if you like, the thigh bone's the strongest bone in the body, so the ambulance man was saying. They call it the femur.'

'You don't say,' Mum said, somewhat uninterested in this detail.

'Yes indeed, hen, you'll be glad to know that apart from that he's absolutely fine.'

'So just to recap then,' Mum said, 'what you're *sayin'* is, he's going to live?'

'Aye, hen, that's right.'

'So you're *sure* it's not fatal?'

'Come come, there's no need for that, hen, don't you worry yourself one wee bit with silly thoughts like that. It would take a lot more than a railway sleeper to get rid of a man like big Joe. He's as strong as an ox, that man!'

Laughlin gave Mum the details of the hospital and Mum thanked him for his trouble and hung up the phone and her disappointment was visible for all the world to see.

Somewhat deflated myself, I picked up my bag from the couch and dragged it behind me on my way to my room. Once I was there, thoughts of my fine Johnny crept into my mind again and it wasn't long before I'd forgotten the disappointment of my da's narrow escape with death. I touched my bag, the same bag my fine Johnny had touched that very afternoon, and I closed my eyes and could see us there together in our very own French château at Fontainebleau, if you don't mind, and I'm wearing my wedding gown of antique lace a hundred seamstresses have stitched by hand and just for me, and the crystal buttons are glinting in the afternoon sun and the scent of French lavender fills the air and I never want this moment to end.

Mum made us a mince and onion curry for our tea that night – well, it's not every day your da narrowly escapes death and gets kept in the hospital. And, my, how we laughed. We told jokes all night long and had the singsongs we could never have when he was there. We put on his Neil Diamond LPs and Andrew sang into the hairbrush and we rustled bags of crisps and crunched out loud and no one told us to 'make less fuckin' noise!'

I went to bed happy that night, but I couldn't sleep. Not even thoughts of my da agonising in his hospital bed with his femur mashed to a pulp could distract me from the pangs of love that Cupid's arrow had been firing at my heart since four o'clock that afternoon. I tossed and turned for hours on end until finally, in the wee small hours, I drifted into a velvety slumber on a bed of soft, red, rose petals, my fine Johnny by my side.

I did my hair the next morning using Mum's curling tongs and added a dab of rouge to my cheeks from her make-up box. When I got to school Leanne noticed all right and told me I looked pretty and what was I looking so pretty for? And my face went bright purple again like those beetroots and Leanne guessed straightaway it must have been about a boy.

The bell rang at five to four. I ran to the toilet and checked how I looked. I don't know who I expected to see but all I got was myself and I looked like I always looked, like shite, and there was nothing I could do. I ran away from the mirror and out into the playground and across the grass you're not supposed to walk on and I squeezed myself through the hole in the railings onto Camper Street and I waited and waited, then I looked up and down the street and I waited some more. Then the darkness came and I knew it was five o'clock 'cause Mr Stewart came out to the front of his shop to close the shutters and turn the key in the door and when he saw me standing at the railings he smiled and called out 'Hello!' from across the street and I raised my hand and called 'Hello!' back but I didn't feel much like smiling. I looked up and down the street one last time and then I picked up my bag and headed for home.

Joan Crawford's lips

Mum used to keep her make-up in a huge box in the bathroom and she used to put her make-up on every day before she did anything else, 'cause Mum said once she had her make-up on, she could face Goliath. When I asked who Goliath was, she told me if I'd gone to the Sunday school instead of watching *Randall and Hopkirk (Deceased)*, then I'd know fine well who he was. Mum had every colour of eyeshadow you could care to imagine in that box and she had lipsticks too, as far as the eye could see, and sometimes me and Izzy would spend hours looking through that box and trying on the different colours. Once I tried on Mum's blue eyeshadow and I looked like Giovanni's wife at the chip shop on the corner and another time Izzy tried on the emerald green and she looked like Mrs Berry the chemistry teacher.

One day when I came home from school Mum wasn't there so I did my homework and when I was finished, I went to the bathroom, took out her make-up box and raked through it, wondering what colours might suit me that day. That's when I found the lipstick called Hollywood Red and it looked just like the lipstick Joan Crawford wore in *Whatever Happened to Baby Jane?*, Mum's favourite movie. I took it out of the box, twisted off the lid and marvelled at the redness, and I ran that creamy lipstick up the inside of my forearm and the redness stood out against my white skin like fresh blood on snow. I held it to my lips to see if it might suit me, then ran it around my lips all the while hoping it might make me look like Joan Crawford. When I was finished I stepped back from the mirror and tilted my head to the side like Mum always did when she finished putting her lipstick on and I stared at my reflection. My Joan Crawford lips looked so good, so glamorous, that I couldn't help but smile and for the first time in my life, I dared think myself beautiful. Then I started to dream about Joan Crawford and I closed my eyes and made a wish that some day I'd be rich and famous too, and that people would queue up at The Roxy to see me on the big screen on a Saturday night with my Hollywood Red lips. And after my movie premieres hundreds of fans would line up and beg me for my autograph and I'd have to say to them, I don't have time just at the minute to be signing photographs, 'cause I've Peter Cushing to meet for a Babycham in the lobby bar.

I had left the door to the bathroom half open and next thing I knew my da was storming in through the front door of the house and when he saw me in the bathroom staring at myself in the mirror wearing my Joan Crawford lips, he pushed the door wide open and told me I was nothing but a filthy fucking whore and to get that muck washed off my fucking face right there and then. Then he stormed out of the bathroom slamming the door behind him. I raced to the door to lock it, then leaned back against it and cried with shame 'cause maybe he was right, maybe I was a filthy whore standing there admiring myself in the mirror thinking I'm Joan Crawford sipping Babychams with Peter Cushing of all people in lobby bars.

I stood up from the bathroom floor and took a piece of toilet paper and tried to rub that Hollywood Red lipstick off, but the colour was so red and so creamy it stuck to my lips like glue and instead of coming off I smudged it all over my mouth and my chin and all the while I cried more tears of shame. That's when Mum arrived home and when she heard my cries she came running. She knocked on the bathroom door and I was too ashamed to come out in case she saw me and thought me a filthy whore too, so I shouted out to her from inside the bathroom that I was okay and waited quietly until I heard her go away. Then I stood in front of the mirror and I scrubbed and scrubbed at my lips until they bled and I tilted my head to the side and stared at my reflection again and the blood-stained lips stared back at me and I vowed I'd never dare think myself beautiful again.

The Bonnie Prince Charlie

My da's pal Harry had a big concrete shed for sale and he offered it dirt cheap to my da who took it straight away and had it put up on our land. Once it was finished a man appeared from the council carrying a clipboard and he asked my da if he had permission to put the shed up and my da told him to fuck right off, else he'd set the dogs on him. The man from the council never came back and so my da used the shed to go into business with his pal Franky, selling wholesale fruit and vegetables to fruit and vegetable shops far and wide.

Franky had been our family friend for years and what a great laugh he was. Whenever he came to our house he'd have us all in stitches with the stories he'd tell, and he was the kind of guy you could talk to about anything and he always made you feel good. Franky was more like family than a friend. That's how great he was.

And then matters started to go wrong in the business. One day my da found out that Franky was stealing money from the bank account and so that night he spoke with Franky on the phone and confronted him about the money. Franky said he wouldn't discuss it on the phone but that my da should meet him in the car park at The Bonnie Prince Charlie pub and that he should come alone.

So my da had a whisky or maybe it was two and when he was finished he put on his jacket and headed to the car. I ran after him 'cause I was worried, and told him I was coming too. As we walked past the shed my da picked up a garden spade and a pair of scissors and that's when I got scared and I asked my da what he was planning to do with a garden spade and a pair of scissors, but he didn't say anything and I wondered what was going to happen that night in that car park at The Bonnie Prince Charlie. We got into the car, me and my da, and just as we were about to turn out of our driveway my da opened the door and threw the garden spade and the scissors behind the gate and said, 'You're right enough, there's no need for that.' And when I heard my da say that I felt relieved and I knew that everything was going to be okay.

It only took us five minutes to drive there and when we arrived I was surprised to see Franky's brother Jack there too and in a way I was glad, 'cause that meant I could have a right good laugh with Jack while Franky and my da sorted out their differences. And as me and my da got out of the car Franky and Jack got out of their car too. I smiled and waved at them, I mean, why wouldn't I?

Franky motioned for my da to follow him to the opposite side of the car park and so I made my way towards Jack so I could have that right good laugh and as I approached I said to Jack, 'I wonder what this is all about, eh?' And Jack might have said something back to me but, to be honest, I don't know. I got distracted by a sound, you see, and I turned around to see where the sound was coming from and that's when I started to shut down and wish I wasn't there.

The sound I'd heard was my da trying to struggle from Franky's grip and I watched Franky as he took my da by the throat and pushed him down on to the gravel. I wanted to scream but nothing came out, like how it happens in dreams sometimes when you're being chased by monsters and you're running as fast as you can, but you're getting nowhere. Time slowed down. I wanted it to move on but time doesn't work like that when bad things are happening. It moves slowly in a defiant way that makes your heart ache for love and safety. I stood still, motionless like the clock on the wall I couldn't see, and next I knew Franky was kneeling on top of my da and holding him down in the gravel with his left hand as his right hand ever so precisely reached behind his back and into the waistband of his trousers where he'd concealed the hammer. I watched Franky as he held the hammer high above his head before bringing it crashing down onto my da's skull and that's when I started to run and my legs were heavy like lead just like in those dreams with the monsters again. I struggled against the lead and I managed to run and I reached Franky and my da just in time for Franky to lay the second blow to my da. My da didn't let out a sound and I knew he was trying to be brave for me and then Franky lifted the hammer again and crashed it down a third time and this time my da did let out a scream and I mean that's nothing to be ashamed of. Sure, other people's daddies get scared sometimes too.

And I didn't know what to do. Sometimes, when I think about it now, I know there were other things I could have done. I mean there was the gravel, I could have picked some up and thrown it in Franky's eyes. I could have picked up one of the big huge rocks that lined the car park and smashed it down on Franky's skull. I could have run to the pub across the road to get help. But then four of the patrons were already standing at the door of the pub watching the horror unfold, sipping on their pints and chatting amongst themselves and none of them came to help me or my da.

In the end, all I could think of was to try to pull Franky off and Franky was a big man, nearly 25 stone Mum said once, and so I stood behind him as he kneeled on my da with his hammer in his hand and I dug my fingers into his temples and I felt his thin white skin come away in my fingernails and that's when Franky turned towards me and held his hammer high above his head and tried to bring it crashing down on my skull so I stepped back out of the way. And then he came at me again with that hammer of his and I backed away a little more, thinking about myself as usual instead of my da who needed me beside him. From my safe distance I watched my da as he lay there, his body recoiled in pain, with the white gravel turning red beneath his head and his mouth wide open, as if screaming in pain. But I didn't hear a sound.

All of a sudden Jack appeared beside Franky, and when I saw Jack's familiar face, the face of our friend who was nearly like family, I knew he had come to help me. But Jack hadn't come to help and I watched him as he took a baseball bat from behind his back and joined his brother as they carried on with their mission. I knew that Jack was ashamed 'cause he couldn't look me in the eye and once he and Franky had dealt enough blows to my da's face and knee caps, it was Jack who called off the assault, screaming to his brother that that was enough now. Then the two of them took off, running to their white Ford Escort, and they left me with my da bleeding into the gravel in the car park at The Bonnie Prince Charlie.

After a week in hospital my da discharged himself – black and blue, broken teeth, walking with a stick – and at the end of the court case the judge ruled it was just two blokes having a barney in a pub car park.

It's all a little hazy and distant now, the memory is fading back into its box for another wee while, and the fear and horror are retreating to that place where they live, lying in wait, and there's a lot of stuff I'll never understand about that night. However, this I do know. I know that I stayed and I watched this happen and although I did the best I could, there's a wee voice inside my head that tells me what I did just wasn't enough. That awful voice reminds me that just as the hammer came towards me I stepped to the side, away from my da, to avoid its blow. And from now until the end of time I'll wish I'd taken that blow to the head, 'cause it would have been one less blow my da would have had to take.

And I'm wondering now if I screamed as all of this was happening, but I doubt if I did. Maybe if I had screamed then, I wouldn't be screaming now.

Brief encounter

One day Nanny took ill and her back was so sore she couldn't find comfort no matter which way she lay and the pain was so bad she couldn't make it down the lane any more. The doctor came and said Nanny would have to have some tests, so Mum took Nanny to the specialist and when the tests were over, the specialist phoned Mum and told her he needed to speak to her straightaway.

I was working in my da's fruit and vegetable shop that day like I had every day since I left school, even though I wished I had a nice job as a secretary putting on high-heeled shoes and Sheer Brazil Nut tights every day of the week. When Mum came back to the shop after speaking with the specialist she had tears in her eyes and she told us that Nanny had cancer in her pancreas, and when I heard that I sat down on the 56-pound sacks of Ayrshire potatoes we'd made up into three-pound bags that morning to sell on the weekend and I held my hands up to my face and wept into them, and just then a customer came into the shop and my da was mad, 'cause it was him who had to go and serve them, while I lay there on the potatoes in tears.

The cancer in Nanny's pancreas got worse while all the unrest was going on at home between Bruce and my da. The doctors said there was nothing they could do for her and that she'd be better off in her own bed at home rather than staring at the white sterile walls of a hospital ward.. When she got home I spent nearly every evening with her in her bedroom with the telly on and some nights we watched our favourite movie, *Brief Encounter*, and Nanny would send Grampa out to Botterill's bottle shop to get a bottle of sweet sherry, 'for the lassies'. Grampa did as he was told and he strolled there slowly, smoking his Embassy Regal as he went, and when he got back with the sherry Mum and I would have a glass but Nanny wouldn't 'cause Nanny never drank a day in her life. Some nights I'd take Cleo our black mongrel in to see Nanny and she'd jump up on Nanny's candlewick bedspread and Nanny would laugh and she'd tell me Cleo was 'skinny like a whippet' and then she'd laugh all the more and Cleo would settle herself down for the night on the bed right between Nanny and me and she'd lick the bedspread in the hope of finding a crumb.

Nanny ended up in so much pain, a nurse had to come and look after her during the nights and the nurse gave Nanny morphine. She told us it was the morphine and not the cancer that would eventually kill Nanny and I didn't know whether to be happy or sad, 'cause I couldn't bear to see Nanny suffer like that and at the same time I couldn't bear to imagine her dead.

Two weeks passed and we knew that the end was near and the nurse said she would have to call an ambulance to come and take Nanny to the hospital. Before the ambulance came the nurse wrapped what was left of Nanny's tiny body in a blanket and the ambulance men gently placed Nanny on a stretcher and took her to the waiting ambulance and Cleo jumped at the stretcher and tried to lick Nanny's hand and Nanny smiled and I knew if she could have, she would have laughed and said that Cleo was 'skinny like a whippet'.

But Nanny had barely the energy to breathe, never mind laugh. Grampa stood and watched the ambulance carry his wife of 60 years away from him and when the ambulance disappeared into the horizon he put on his jacket, lit up an Embassy Regal and walked down to Botterill's to get a bottle of sweet sherry in 'for the lassies', 'cause he knew that's what Nanny would have wanted.

The doctor at the hospital put an oxygen mask on Nanny so she could breathe a little easier and they gave her more morphine to try to ease her pain. Bruce and my da joined me and Mum and Grampa at Nanny's bedside that night during the visiting hour and even though she was weak, she lifted her finger and pointed to each and every one of us and told us that she hoped her suffering meant that none of us would ever have to suffer the same agony in our own lives and of course she included my da in that and why wouldn't she, she was the kindest, most generous woman I've ever known. And she told my da and Bruce to sort out their differences, that she wanted them to make up and to talk again and my da stood there like a wee boy in the headmaster's office with his head hung low and he agreed he'd make an effort just for her.

Nanny died the next day while I was having my tooth filled at Dr Dunn's the dentist on the Glasgow Road. Had I known she would pass away at three o'clock that afternoon, I would have rubbed my tooth with oil of cloves and ignored the pain that had kept me awake for half the night, but I didn't, and so I missed Nanny's last moments on earth and my last chance to tell her how much I had loved her.

Later that night me and Cleo went next door to Nanny's house and into her bedroom and the room felt sad and bare, like when you take down the Christmas tree and the fairy lights twelve days after Christmas. I put the telly on and slotted in Nanny's copy of *Brief Encounter* and I played our movie one last time and I thought about Nanny and how I didn't get to say goodbye to her, not really, not properly, and I wished I could have those days back again, just Nanny, me and Cleo up on the candlewick bedspread with a wee glass of sherry in my hand. As I sat on the bed I stroked Cleo's head and told her how much I had loved Nanny and how much I learnt from her and Cleo licked the pillow where Nanny's head had been, 'cause she missed Nanny too.

With Nanny gone the days seemed long and sometimes I made the trip myself down the cobbled laneway to the market where Nanny spent nearly every day, just to listen to the hustle and bustle. Sometimes I imagined Nanny there beside me as I raked through Jessie's jumpers and cardigans and one day Jessie asked me if I was interested in any bras and briefs she'd just got in at five pounds the set and I thanked her very much and told her I wasn't in the market for bras and briefs that day. Then I went past Whistling Tommy's stall and remembered the time Nanny was searching for catering-sized pickled gherkins for Maria the art teacher and I couldn't remember if she'd ever got them.

I walked around for hours in the lane wearing my beanie and my winter coat and I thought about Nanny all the while and how much I missed her and as I wandered further up the lane I saw a drunk man begging, his trousers in tatters and his shoes with no soles, and as I walked past him I pulled out a couple of coins from the pocket of my winter coat and placed them discreetly in his out-held hand.

Bruce and my da kept the promise they'd made to Nanny to try to get along, but still my da refused to sign over the title deeds to Bruce's bungalow. Finally, with much to-ing and fro-ing with me as the messenger, my da agreed to sign over the title deeds to the old cottage that we used to live in before we built the bungalows and that title deed included a tiny portion of my da's two-and-a-half acres and on that tiny portion stood the greenhouses where Rusty and Silver used to live.

The living arrangements for Grampa and Bruce were quite cramped in their new home but it was better than before. Now they owned the house they slept in and they set up a little business in the greenhouses selling plants and herbs. Bruce and Grampa knew everything there was to know about every plant and herb they sold and people came from miles around to ask their advice.

Slowly, Bruce started to feel better about life and he painted his living-room walls lilac again and this time we didn't laugh 'cause we knew that Bruce wasn't just artistic, but a man whose heart knew forgiveness and Bruce was Nanny's son if ever there was one.

So in the end my da got his dream to keep the title deeds to both the semi-detached bungalows and some days he strutted up and down his land just for the pleasure of it, like lord of the fucking manor. And the bastard slept like a baby every night in the week.

167

The longest knife in the cutlery drawer

Andrew was angry. About everything. Angry about being my da's son; about the way my da treated Mum, me, Izzy, Nanny, Grampa and Bruce; angry about the way he treated our animals; angry about a lifetime of being shouted at morning, noon and night. And the anger ate away at him bit by bit, until there was almost nothing left of him and he arrived at an anonymous destination, a place where he didn't know who he was anymore, and by that time, anyway, he didn't care.

So Andrew went from being a lovely wee laddie baking potatoes in bonfires with Donald next door, to being a dreadlocked troubled soul who popped pills, snorted speed, sniffed amyl nitrate and smoked dope night after night after night.

Andrew had no way of supporting himself so he still lived at home under my da's roof and every morning my da reminded him of that fact when he got up at five o'clock in the morning to get ready for work and he'd start banging on Andrew's bedroom door, shouting and screaming about how lazy Andrew was and how if he didn't get up right there and then, there would be hell to pay. But what my da didn't realise was that Andrew was already in hell, and getting out of bed wasn't going to change anything.

My da banned all of Andrew's friends from coming to the house to see Andrew, what with them looking like a bunch of lazy bastards with long untidy hair and no jobs, so Andrew just told his pals to come around to the back of the house late at night and climb in his bedroom window if they wanted to see him, which they did. Rory Corr was the only one who didn't have to come and go by Andrew's bedroom window. We all liked Rory, even my da tolerated him, which was really saying something 'cause Rory had long hair and a dope habit unsurpassed by anybody else in our town. The difference with Rory was that he had a job. Whenever Rory came to our place he'd just walk in through the front door and he'd shout out, 'Awright, Betty, are you in?' And Mum would be in the kitchen and she'd shout back, 'Aye, I'm in, Rory. I'm in the kitchen! Come on through and I'll put an egg and a slice of bacon in the pan fur yae!' And Rory would make his way to the kitchen and slap his egg and slice of bacon between two pieces of white sliced bread and butter, then he'd make himself a cup of tea and chat to Mum for a while before he made his way to Andrew's room to wake him up, which was no mean feat, 'cause Andrew didn't even want to be alive, never mind be woken up.

Rory painted buildings for a living. Sometimes he painted in the local banks when they were shut at night and whenever he had a big job like that on he'd ask Andrew to come and help him, 'cause Andrew was big and strong. Rory would come to our place in the afternoon before the job was to start and after he'd had his cup of tea and bacon and eggs on two slices of bread and butter he'd head to Andrew's room to try to wake him up.

'Come on, Andy, I've got a bank job on tonight. Are you comin' to help me?'

And Andrew would tell Rory to fuck off and go and paint his own banks, then he'd roll back over and fall asleep.

The years went by and nothing changed, my da still shouted morning, noon and night about everything and nothing, and Andrew, well, he was numb to it all by now and he resigned himself to thinking that that's just how life was and, sadly, he thought he had no means of ever getting out of the situation he was in. So he stayed there, at home under my da's fucking roof, and it wouldn't have surprised me if one day Rory went into Andrew's room and found Andrew dead right there on the polished floor.

But that never happened. In fact, some years later it was Rory who was found dead, not in Andrew's room, but on the floor of a tenement flat in Glasgow's southside. They say he died of an overdose and that came as no surprise, 'cause Rory had a fierce drug habit that would have put most to shame.

Eventually Andrew stopped snorting speed and popping pills and all he did from time to time was smoke a little dope. He even managed to get his own wee council flat in Garthamlock and sometimes he'd sit in his flat late at night by himself and think of all the wrongs my da had done and one night it all got too much for him and he decided to do something about it. So he armed himself with the longest knife he could find in his cutlery drawer and he made his way to my da's house, crossing fields in the middle of the black night while the rain blew horizontally and soaked him to the skin and he couldn't have cared less.

Mum was at the kitchen sink when she looked out the window and saw the shape of something moving through the fields towards the house. She didn't think much about it until the shape got closer and she could see it was Andrew and that's when she glanced at the clock and saw it was close to ten o'clock and what was Andrew doing crossing fields at this time of night in the rain? A panic set in her as she raced to the back door. Andrew was already standing there waiting for her to open it and he was clutching his knife, and he had a faraway look in his eye.

'What are you doing, son?' she said.

'I've come to kill the bastard,' Andrew said, pushing past Mum to come inside. 'I cannae fuckin' take the torment any longer. The way he's treated you, Ali and Izzy – the way he treated Nanny, Grampa and Bruce. I cannae fuckin' stand it any longer, do you understand?'

'Aye, son, of course I understand. But the bastard's no' worth swinging for! Do *you* understand?'

'I don't care if I have to spend the rest of my life locked up, Mum. I'll happily do the time. I just want the pleasure of cutting his fuckin' throat and making him pay the price, so get out of my way, I'm going through to do it now!'

'But he's in the good room watching the telly, son. Please don't do it, Andrew, *please* I beg you. Go home and think about what it is you're about to do and think about what it'll do to me if you go through with it.'

Mum stood in the doorway to the red carpeted hallway that would lead Andrew to my da in the good room, barricading his way with her body. Andrew tried to push past her and through her tears Mum begged him again not to do it and asked him wasn't it already bad enough that we'd all gone through this hell with the bastard, without one of us ending up in jail? Andrew was still clutching his knife as Mum begged and his hands were shaking and Mum looked him in the eye and begged him some more and in the end his own eyes filled with tears and he dropped his knife, the longest one he could find in his cutlery drawer, and it landed on the floor. Mum bent down slowly and picked it up.

'Mum, I love you,' Andrew sobbed, 'and I don't want to hurt you any more than you've already been hurt. But my anger won't go away. It's just there all the time, burning a hole in my gut while that prick sits in his good room watching his fuckin' gameshows none the wiser, and it's all of us who carry the burden.'

'I know, son, I know,' Mum said gently, pushing the wet dreadlocks from his forehead and in behind his ears, 'but it's us who have the bigger shoulders and we can afford to carry that burden. Some day, Andrew, we'll sort everything out and we'll look back on these times and we'll laugh 'cause we'll be free. Free from him and the pain he's put us through and your anger'll disappear son, I promise you.'

While Andrew sobbed some more Mum rocked him in her arms like he was still her wee boy, and he told her again that he loved her then he turned and left and made his way in the dark through the fields again and he took his time, 'cause he was in no rush. And he was sorry he didn't cut my da's throat that night, but there would be other nights, and the thought of that consoled him. Just then the black sky opened up again and the rain came lashing down harder than before and Andrew was soaked through to the skin again and still he didn't care.

All the while my da sat in his good room watching his gameshow and when the adverts came on, he walked down the red carpeted hallway that led him to the kitchen and he opened the door and stood in the doorway, the same doorway that Mum had barricaded only moments before to save his life, and demanded she pour him another fucking whisky. And Mum went to the fridge and poured his whisky, more whisky than water, just the way he liked it, and she wondered why she'd stopped Andrew after all.

Swinging in the gentle breeze

My da's mother, Helen, had just come home from picking up the weekly groceries from the village store and as she pulled into the driveway she could see that stupid dog Rex sitting outside the barn door whimpering and fidgeting, unable to sit at peace, and she thought that maybe it was worms that were causing him to fidget like that. She got out of the car and lifted all the bags of groceries out of the boot with one hand and headed to the house and called to Rex, 'Come away from that barn door, ya stupit wee bastard! Come and get your bone.' Rex looked towards her, but he didn't budge, just sat there with one ear sat straight up in the wind and one ear folded forward covering half his right eye.

She took the shopping into the house and reappeared a few minutes later with Rex's bone in her hand. 'What the fuck are you doing up there at that barn door?' she yelled. 'Come down here now and get your fuckin' bone!' But still Rex didn't move. Stubborn wee bastard, she thought as she walked up the slope to the front of the barn door and put the bone down in front of him.

'Right, here's your fuckin' bone.' She placed it at his feet and Rex wouldn't even look at it. 'What the fuck is wrong with you?' she said as she bent down to stroke him behind the ear that was standing up in the wind and all the while she thought it was weird 'cause normally he'd knock her over in the rush to get his weekly bone. Rex started to bark and jump at the barn door. Helen had never seen him behave like this. 'What wrong wi' you, Rex?' she said. 'You want inside the barn now, is that it?' So with all her might Helen slid the door wide open and the daylight rushed in, chasing out the darkness, and particles of hay hung effortlessly in the beams of sunlight that shone on a sight she would rather not have seen.

He'd dressed himself in his good suit and the shirt and tie she'd bought him for Christmas the year before from Marks & Spencer's, and he seemed much smaller now in death. She was surprised that those were her only thoughts as she stood there at the barn door, watching him swing in the gentle breeze that blew in from the potato fields they'd planted together only the season before. And then she thought about that day, as she watched him swing, and remembered how he'd accused her of being a useless, good-for-nothing, lazy cow and how she'd wished him dead right there and then.

They'd had seven kids, him and Helen, and he'd shown more care and respect for his Rover 3000 than he ever did for my da. He garaged that car come rain, hail or shine, and polished it religiously every Sunday with turtle wax and a nice soft chamois leather from the car accessory shop in town.

He had driven to see the doctor that day. Later the doctor told Helen that the cancer was everywhere and that he had told my da's da that he was sorry, but there was nothing he could do. My da's da thanked the doctor for his time then drove himself home and carefully parked his pride and joy in the barn. Then he went inside the house and dressed himself in his Sunday best before making his final journey back to the barn where he covered his most-beloved possession with a blanket to protect her before climbing on top of her to reach the rafters that would secure the rope that would see an end to all the pain and inconvenience that cancer brings.

Helen turned slowly away from the barn door and took Rex in her arms as she headed back towards the house. Just before she reached her front door she noticed the cows lying down in the fields across the way and she knew that that meant the rain was coming and that she'd have to get the washing off the line. But the washing could wait. Before she turned the handle of the door to go inside, she turned around and looked back towards the barn and the rafters creaked in the breeze, and she called out his name

177

and held her hand up in the breeze as if she were waving goodbye. Then she turned and sat down on the cold concrete doorstep and held her head in her hands and the tears trickled down her wrists and into her sleeves.

Diagnosed one minute, dead the next

It went so fast. It was like he was diagnosed one minute and dead the next.

We weren't close to my da's side of the family, although we used to visit them every Sunday when we were wee and while we were there they never once spoke to us, or about us, except on the odd occasion when they'd feign interest and ask my da to remind them of our names again. But mostly they'd talk to my da about tractors and potatoes and the brake pads on their Rover 3000 and sometimes they talked about the increase in the price of tomatoes whenever the rains fell heavy in Tenerife.

My da's mother baked her own fairy cakes and sometimes when we went there she'd put the fairy cakes with the frosted pink icing on a white china plate on the table in front of us, but we didn't dare touch one single cake for fear of my da telling us to mind our manners. So we'd just stare at the frosted pink icing for half an hour hoping somebody would tell us to help ourselves, but no one ever did.

When we got older we stopped going to visit them every Sunday and they remained the strangers they had always been. I felt nothing when it was announced that my da's da had cancer. Mum and I were busying ourselves in the gift shop my da had bought cheap on the Glasgow Road that day, unpacking the boxes of bric-a-brac we'd just bought at the wholesalers, and every so often Mum would open a box and pull out something like a porcelain fish that doubled as a barometer and she'd say, 'What did we buy this for? We'll never sell this shite!' But actually she was wrong. We always sold that shite.

Next, the front door of the shop burst open and my da rushed in, wailing like a mad man, tears running down his face and his eyes searching for a place to run to where he could retain his dignity and hide his pain. Mum ran out from behind the counter and took a hold of him and she wrapped him in her arms and asked him to tell her what had happened. For moments he could only sob and hide his face behind his hands and I felt his embarrassment at being seen like that by me, so I turned away and stuck the price tags on the porcelain fish and pretended not to notice.

Again Mum asked my da to tell her what had happened but he could barely speak. He sobbed from way deep down inside of himself and every so often he paused to wipe his nose on his sleeve and eventually his sobbing slowed and he prepared himself to say it.

'He's hung himself,' he said.

Mum went pale as she took my da in her arms and walked with him to the darkness of the storeroom at the back of the shop where he wouldn't be seen like this by anyone, and pulled the door shut tight behind her. I heard his limp body slump against the door and slide down to the ground and I heard his cries of pain, the likes of which I hope I'll never hear again. I could hear Mum comfort him and for the first time he let himself be comforted by her, her of all people, her that he abused on every occasion that he could and here she was offering love and safety and tenderness and that made him feel even worse.

He allowed himself to be comforted for five minutes more and not one minute longer and when his time was up, he disentangled himself from the warmth of Mum's embrace and pulled the storeroom door open announcing that he had work to do, that this was no time to be behaving in such a way. He dusted himself down, took a deep breath, stormed past me like he always did, and, without stopping nor looking me in the eye, asked me what price I had put on the porcelain fish. So I told him and he told me that was way too cheap for an ornament so fine. And with that he disappeared out of the shop and the door closed behind him with a bang.

Mum tries to kill my da using out-of-date tranquillizers

The clock finally struck five. Mum had never been a clock-watcher since she started her wee part-time job as nursing assistant at the local hospital, but tonight was different. Tonight there was something worth heading home for and as she raced past big Janet, the sister in charge, she yelled good night only to have Janet race after her and beg her to take old Bessie to the toilet before she left. Ah, fuck it, Mum thought, but unable to say no, she about turned and frogmarched old Bessie to the toilet, pulled down her big sensible knickers, eased her slowly down onto the toilet seat and chatted idly to her as they both waited for nature to take its course. When it was over Mum bent over and wiped Bessie's arse with the harsh hospital-grade toilet paper and sprinkled some talcum powder in her crack and returned her, relieved and dignified, to her chair in the day room that was filled with unsuspecting roommates and visitors alike. Mission accomplished, Mum ran like a mad woman to the locker room, grabbed her fake Burberry raincoat and matching handbag she'd got at the Marie Curie Cancer Shop on the Glasgow Road, and ran out into the torrential rain.

It had been torrential for days and just wouldn't let up. Mum held her raincoat high above her head as she ran from the safety of Ward 27, splashing her way across the car park and avoiding the potholes like she was dancing through a field of land mines. Finally she jumped into the car, relieved. 'Aaaah, thank Christ. I made it,' she said out loud as she put the key in the ignition, turned on the cassette player and slipped in her favourite recording of Michael Crawford singing 'Phantom of the Opera'. She'd bought the tape twelve years before and she listened to it every day and never tired of it. Track one started up as she pulled out of the hospital grounds and headed off into the dark night with the window wipers on maximum, headlights full beam, and Michael's voice for company on the dark and lonely journey home.

Track seven was just about to start as she turned off the dirt track and crunched up the pebble driveway. She could see a light on in the lounge room. 'Ah, fuck it, he's back already,' she thought, and she switched off the tape player as the car came to a halt and the three dogs inside the house stuck their wet noses through the pussy flap desperate for her to come inside. Mum ejected Michael from the cassette player and placed him in his cassette

183

cover before slotting him gently in the glove box on top of
Boy George's Greatest Hits and the twelve-inch disco remix
cassette version of 'Saddle up and ride your Pony'. She
gathered her bag and raincoat and raced to the house, less
apprehensive of the future now, in fact more hopeful than
she'd ever been. And the rain was still pouring down.

'I wonder if it will ever stop,' she said quietly to
herself.

She'd no sooner thrown her coat and bag down on the
kitchen table when he started yelling for her to get him a
fucking whisky. And, without thinking, she prepared it,
more whisky than water, just the way he liked it, and she
delivered it to him in his leather armchair in the good
room and the dogs followed her along the red carpeted
hallway as far as the good-room door and waited patiently
outside for her to come back out. He grabbed the whisky
from her hand and downed it in one and thrust the empty
glass back into her hand.

'Fill it up – and less water this time,' he growled. She
made her way back to the kitchen followed by the dogs
who stuck their wet noses up her skirt and tickled her
arse, and she bent down in the kitchen and cuddled each
one of them. And then she turned back to the fridge and
made him his drink and took it back to him. He held out
his hand without taking his eyes off his gameshow on the
telly, grabbed the drink from her and downed it in one,
then tossed the empty glass in the air and Mum watched

it fall in slow motion, like she was in a dream. And all the while he paid no attention to her, reminding her of her invisibility. Sure, all she was good for was filling up his glass, cooking his meals and picking up his skid-marked underpants from the toilet floor and soaking them in a bucket of bleach. Then he barked that he wanted his dinner and so back she went down the corridor to the kitchen and started to prepare it. Once the potatoes were boiling and the fish was simmering she pulled from her handbag the small glass bottle that Martha at the hospital had given her before she died. 'They worked a treat for me, Betty,' Martha had said. 'Mind you, they're out of date now, but try them anyway. What have you got to lose?'

'Martha's right, I've got nothing to lose,' Mum reassured herself as she set about crushing ten of the tranquillizers between two spoons. And as she crushed them, her mind started wandering to that night not so long ago when Andrew had wanted to do the job she was about to do now and she'd stopped him and now she couldn't think why.

As the potatoes came to the boil she dipped her finger in the water and tasted it to make sure there was enough salt. How she could dip her finger into a pot of boiling water and not feel anything is anybody's guess, but then she lived in a pot of constantly boiling water and hadn't felt a thing for the whole of her married life to him. But today there was light at the end of the tunnel and she felt excited, Christ she felt *something*, and she caught herself singing her favourite piece from *The Phantom* where there's a great crescendo and Michael gets all passionate and goes up into his high voice. Whenever she listened to that part while she was driving she'd turn up the volume, and if she was stopped at the traffic lights she'd roll down the windows and let the sound escape for the benefit and enjoyment of the passers-by.

Mum took the potatoes from the stove and drained them in the colander, then put the finishing touches to the mornay sauce and poured it over the slice of grilled lemon sole she'd picked up at the fish shop earlier in the day during her tea break. Then she took the potato masher from the kitchen drawer, added a chunk of butter to the pot of drained potatoes and stood there, with the masher in her hand, and took a deep breath. She contemplated the crushed tranquillizers still on the spoon and knew she could back out now if she really wanted to. With no hesitation she held the spoon over the steaming pot of potatoes and let the crushed powder fall slowly into it. And she savoured every moment, one crushed molecule for every moment of pain she'd ever suffered at his hands, and as it entered the pot the molecules began to dissolve and she set about mashing slowly at first, then she built up speed until finally she was mashing frantically, adding milk, more butter and salt as she went. When she was finally convinced that all the evidence had been dissolved she spooned the mashed potato alongside the lemon sole and added a sprig of continental parsley. 'Presentation is everything', that's what Mum used to say.

My da started shouting for Mum to hurry up with his fucking dinner and she yelled out from the kitchen that she was coming and then she made her way down the red carpeted hall and handed him his dinner plate. He surveyed the dish for a split second then started by eating most of the mashed potato in one go and Mum sat down on the chair opposite and waited. She watched him eat every mouthful of that potato and she didn't take her eyes off him for fear of missing the moment where he'd slip into a coma and she'd get peace for the night, if not the rest of her life. And she waited and watched him and nothing happened. Then she waited and watched some more and still no joy. She waited and watched for so long that her own eyes started getting heavier and the more she fought the heavier they got until finally Mum keeled over on the chair and dozed off, snoring away right there in front of him with her head tilted back and her mouth wide open like she was catching flies. And my da looked up from his dinner and started yelling at her to get up off her fat lazy arse and get him a fucking whisky. He may as well have yelled at the wall for all the good it did, 'cause Mum was out for the count and there was nothing he could do.

Cock-a-leekie

Mum kept lacing my da's dinners with Martha's out-of-date tranquillizers until her stock ran out. Then one night as she sat at the kitchen table reading the latest copy of *Your Health And You*, she came across an article talking about the dangers of a high cholesterol diet and how you had to avoid creamy sauces and animal fats and custards and puddings and all the food my da loved and suddenly Mum's future looked rosy again. Of course she had considered other alternatives like having him bumped off by a hit man when he left the pub drunk one night, or waiting until he was in his bed asleep and then sneaking in and covering his entire body from top to toe in nicotine patches. But once she'd pulled off the nicotine patches prior to the arrival of the police his once hairy body would be covered in perfectly square bald patches and how are you going to explain that to the coroner?

No, this dangerously high cholesterol diet seemed like the perfect solution and so Mum set about it straightaway. Feeling happier than she had for a long time Mum put her Michael Crawford *Phantom of the Opera* tape into the tape deck and the music filled the nooks and crannies of every room and once again her heart was filled with hope, just as it had been when she was lacing his dinners with Martha's out-of-date tranquillizers.

Mum's trips to the supermarket started to take a little longer as she loaded up her trolley with dairy products and ten-litre drums of animal fat, and my da was none the wiser and tucked in to everything that Mum prepared and sometimes he even licked his plate clean, it tasted that good.

Izzy was studying law at Aberdeen University at that time and on one of her weekends home we sat at the kitchen table and watched Mum as she poured the contents of a one-litre carton of cream into the pot of cock-a-leekie soup she was preparing for my da.

'Mum, do you think what you're doing is ethical?' Izzy asked.

'Do I think *what* is ethical?'

'Deliberately trying to increase another human being's cholesterol levels for your own gain? I mean, you could go to jail for that kind of behaviour.'

'Ethical? Don't fuckin' talk to me about ethical! Do you think it's ethical that he shouts and screams from morning till night and still dictates his orders to me like I'm his fuckin' slave? Do you think it's ethical that there are times when I can't pay all the bills that come in, but there's always whisky in the house? Do you think it's ethical that he terrorised the life out of my own mother and father before they died? Do you think it's ethical that he refused to give Bruce the title deeds to the house he sweated blood to build? Do you think it's ethical that he abused the animals you brought home and kicked your very own puppy to death right there in front of your eyes? Ethical? Don't talk to me about fuckin' ethical!'

'Okay, okay, I get your point, just so long as this doesn't come back and bite you.'

'Izzy, I don't care if it does come back and bite me. Things have changed. Now I'd happily swing for that bastard and I'll do everything I can to make us all free from him some day.'

'Sure, Mum, it would be great to be free, but does he *really* have to die for that to happen?'

'No, he doesn't *absolutely* have to die, but it would make me happy if he did.'

'All right, do what you like, but it sounds like I might have to defend you on a premeditated murder charge some day.'

'Well, I've thought that through and I think they'll reduce it to manslaughter and if I do end up inside, I'm going to do a degree in Forensic Science by distance learning, I hear it's a helluva interesting course. But anyway, Izzy, you'll not have to defend my innocence 'cause I'll proudly plead guilty and anybody that knows your da would understand why I did it.'

'Well, if you're happy with what you're doing, Mum, I won't stand in your way.'

'Good, and keep your fingers crossed for me. He's on his way right now for his medical to get his HGV licence renewed, so hopefully I'll get good news this afternoon about his cholesterol levels.'

'Aye, fingers crossed, eh Mum?' I said, smiling at the prospect of my da having a massive heart attack in the not too-distant future.

Later in the afternoon my da's lorry pulled into the drive and my da jumped out of the cabin and made his way to the house in a light jog across the field. Mum and I looked at each other. We'd never seen him do a light jog before and he opened the door to the house and breezed into the kitchen beaming from ear to ear.

'Well, that's confirmed,' he said. 'The doctor cannae remember ever seeing anybody healthier than myself in a long time. He says my diet must be fantastic. My cholesterol level is low, my blood pressure is normal – so you'll all be delighted to know, I'm as fit as a fuckin' fiddle!'

All of our faces fell as he made his way in another light jog through the kitchen and up the stairs to the bathroom to have a shower, and I turned to Mum and said, 'How does that work? After all your effort! After all that dairy produce! All that animal fat!'

'Fucked if I know how it works, Ali, hen. Pass me another litre of cream.'

Oh no, my da's no' got cancer

Izzy moved to Australia first, well, she's always been more adventurous than me. I was in my thirties and still living in Scotland when she moved and the burdens of the past weighed me down like a sack of Maris Piper potatoes around my neck. And I'd had enough of that. I wanted a change. I wanted to wake up in the morning and love my life and I couldn't do that stuck in such close proximity to my da and all of the black memories that go along with that. So I jumped on a plane and I joined Izzy, and it's such a long way away, Australia, it seemed like I sat on that plane forever, but all the while I was happy, knowing with each passing minute I was another few kilometres further away from my da and closer to the freedom I thought Australia would bring.

When I finally landed, I walked out of the terminal building and into my new life where the jaggy yellow sun has nothing to do all day but dazzle your eyes and shine on your milk-bottle skin turning it pink. And it wasn't long before I discovered the cold black thoughts I thought I was leaving behind in Scotland had followed me here.

The first few years I lived in Sydney I hated Scotland and I was thankful with every day that passed that I was as far away from the place as I could possibly be. Then one day, out of the blue, I woke up and realised that actually it wasn't Scotland I hated, but the memories of my past there, and that's when my thoughts started to lighten and slowly I let the orange rays of the sun warm my cold black thoughts and I started to think fondly again of tartan kilts and snow-capped mountains and Johnny Frost's patterns on the inside of the windows in the mornings and I think that's maybe when I started to forgive my da a little too.

It was during those first few years in Sydney that Thomas appeared in my life, much like the ice-cream cone reward you might get on a Sunday when you're wee and you've washed the dishes, including the pots, all week long. Thomas was born and bred in Paris and he left France ten years earlier when he was only twenty.

I met him at a friend's dinner party and of course I fell in love with him the moment I saw him with his warm brown eyes and olive skin and jet-black hair all the way to his shoulders and I hoped that one day he would love me too. That night after our baked Alaskas, he invited me to see *Forrest Gump* with him at the pictures the next weekend and things just grew from there. Thomas's love

wrapped me up in the safest place I'd ever known and six
weeks after our first date I moved into his apartment. Four
months later we were married.

Twelve years on we're still married and Thomas is my
rock, the kindest and most tender man I've ever known.
Thomas who lies on my cold side of the bed in winter
to take the chill away before I get into the bed myself.
And sometimes while he's still lying on my side, I pull
back the covers and carefully lie on top of him, for fear of
my skin touching the cold cotton sheets, and once they're
warmed, Thomas slides out from under me and onto his
own side that's still icy cold to the touch and I lie down
on the warmth that he's left behind and if that's not love,
then I don't know what is.

Thomas helped me get back the confidence I must
surely once have had. A day doesn't go by but he's
complimenting me on how smart I am, when all I ever feel
is daft. He tells me every day how beautiful I am, when all
I can think about is the shame of my Joan Crawford lips.
He tells me I couldn't cook the noodles of South East Asia
to save my life, but I'm creative and funny and great to be
with and sometimes I wonder if we're talking about the
same person.

Secure in Thomas's love my mind drifted back to all
those years ago when I locked my banana box away in the
attic and to the promise I made myself that there would
be no more time for fun and careless moments, pushing

stupid stuffed animals on wheels up and down the street. But now, with Thomas by my side, I no longer feared having fun. Instead, I finally knew that I deserved it. So that day, as I sat on my stripy deckchair under the jaggy yellow sun in Sydney, I closed my eyes and took myself back to the attic.

The attic smelled of damp dogs and brown seaweed and skinny rays of squashed sunlight squeezed in through the cracks in the slate roof. I crouched down to avoid banging my head on the sloping roof and I shuffled further in. From the corner of my eye I saw my crocus bowl with 'Plant Use Only' stamped on the side, discarded and lying upside down in a corner. And then my eyes fell on it, my beautiful banana box, sitting in the same spot I'd left it all those years ago, waiting patiently for me to come back as if it always knew I would. I crouched further down and blew away the thick layer of dust that had gathered on the top over the years. When I lifted the lid, wily spiders that had lived there all this time eating daft flies that dared to come too close, scurried for cover. Inside my box, I saw the precious wheel from Molly my Airedale Terrier and one by one the memories of the red handle and the track marks and the fingerprints in the black tar softened by the afternoon sun came back to me and I sat in my stripy deckchair in Sydney with my eyes still closed and smiled. With the warmth of the memories came the heartache of the past too, but I reminded myself that life was different now, I had Thomas in my life, and my heart was stronger than before. Isn't it true, love changes everything?

With my eyes still closed, I brought my banana box and myself back from the attic in Scotland to the safety of my stripy deckchair in Sydney. I opened my eyes, ready to have fun again, but had no idea where to start. Looking for inspiration I picked up a brochure from my local community centre and flicked through it for hours on end. That's when I stumbled on 'Pottery for beginners' and I smiled as I recalled the pottery course Grampa had done when he was 80 years old and the misshapen ashtrays he filled the house with and the clay plates he made and painted with pictures of wild horses galloping through the prairies of Lithuania, not to mention the crumpled plant pots that leaned to the side much like the Leaning Tower of Pisa does.

I enrolled, excited, and waited impatiently for the first day of the course to arrive. Once the class was underway though, I discovered I was shite at pottery and knew instantly how Grampa's garden shed ended up packed to the hilt with plant pots that even the Italians couldn't turn into a tourist attraction. I didn't go back for week two. Somewhat deflated, I flicked through the brochure again. My eyes lit up when I saw 'Singing for beginners' and thought maybe I could relive the Lena Zavaroni aspirations I had as a child. I enrolled but discovered that actually I was shite at singing too. Next I tried 'Watercolours for beginners', closely followed by 'Classical guitar for beginners', then 'The noodles of South East Asia and how to cook them'. And I was shite at all of them.

Then, one day, after enrolling in 'Yoga for beginners', I had a call from the college to advise that the yoga class was unfortunately full and would I like to try something else?

'What else is available?' I asked.

'Well, there's a few spaces left in "Creative writing for beginners".'

'Are you sure I can't get a refund, I mean it's not my fault the yoga class is full.'

'Sorry, Alison, college policy, no refunds. But, wait, if you're not keen on the creative writing course, how about stamp collecting – there's about 150 places left on that course. Would you like me to put you down for that instead?'

'Hmm. Can I think about it overnight?'

'No, I'm sorry. The deadline for all enrolments is today.'

'Bloody hell. All right, just put me down for the creative writing. I'll give it a go.'

On the first night of that course our teacher Dean asked us all to introduce ourselves and to tell the group what had brought us to the course. I stood up and told the group I'd enrolled in loads of other courses and that I'd hated all of them and based on this pattern it was highly unlikely I'd show up for week two. Dean didn't seem to mind that answer at all, in fact he told me he hoped he would see me for week two and inside my head I'm thinking, I doubt it.

He gave us some homework that night for the following week and he gave us a subject to write about but we didn't have to stick to it, for there were no rules in this writing game, at least that's what Dean said. And he gave us tips along the way and one of those was to write every day, come hell or high water, 'cause 'it's the process of writing that makes you a writer'. I had no idea what to write so I called Andrew in Scotland. What with him writing songs all day I was sure he'd be able to help.

I was lucky to catch Andrew on the phone, what with the time difference between Australia and Scotland, and I got him as he was driving along the M8 motorway to Duntocher.

'Awright, Blinky!' he shouted down the phone at me, competing against the noise of the motorway traffic and Radio Scotland's Gaelic FM that he had blaring through the speakers, 'What's happenin'?'

'It's all happenin', Nobbie,' I shouted back, my voice insignificant amongst the bagpipes and the heuchin' and teuchin' that was going on in the car as he sped along. Andrew calls me Blinky and I call him Nobbie – I don't know why, it's just always been that way. Nobbie has its origins in knob – you know, from the noun, 'to be a right knob', and of course it's a term of endearment, I mean you know how it is between families on the West coast of Scotland, or maybe you don't. You should have seen us laugh when Andrew came to visit us in Australia and we came across Nobby's Nuts in the nibbles section at the supermarket and as if the name wasn't funny enough, their slogan 'Nibble Nobby's Nuts' had us splitting our sides.

'What are you up to, darlin'?' I shouted down the phone just as big Boaby McTavish, the guest accordionist on Radio Scotland's Gaelic FM, played the final chord in 'Oh, bonny Mary come muck out the byre with me'.

'I'm on my way down to the studio to practise these wee songs I finished writin' this week. I've got a few session musicians comin' and there's a record company comin' as well to check me out, so fingers crossed they know good music when they hear it, eh? So, tell me, Blinky, how're things?'

'Aye, everything's good,' I said. 'Except I've started this writing course and we have to write a wee somethin' for next week and read it out to the class and I haven't a clue what to write. By the way, while I remember, have you heard our da might have cancer?'

'Well, I hadn't heard a sausage since he attacked me with that iron bar and I got the court order out against him, then just the other day Bruce told me he'd heard something about him having cancer and I thought you fuckin' beauty, there is a God – after all that shite he's put us through. So, what have you heard?'

'Well, Bruce rang me the other week and he was telling

me that big John Brown had been in at the garden centre to buy a few plants for his herbaceous border and while he was there he mentioned to Bruce that he'd heard my da had cancer.'

'And what did Bruce say to big John?' Andrew asked, impatient to hear some seriously bad news.

'Well, apparently Bruce just asked him if he wanted to buy a few petunias for his terracotta tubs and John said a'right and then he told John that'd be eight pound ninety-five and did he want a carrier bag.'

'Naw, what did Bruce say to big John about my da having cancer?'

'Oh, apparently Bruce just told him he wasn't interested in whether my da had cancer or not and had he considered planting some daffodils to add a splash of colour to his front lawn. He's having a hard time shifting those daffodils, or so he was saying.'

'Aye, it's true, daffodils are always hard to shift, especially at the tail end of the season. Well, maybe the rumour's true about him right enough then, Blinky,' Andrew said. 'And I don't mind telling you, when I heard the rumour I did a cancer dance all night long – fuckin' rained non-stop the whole of the next day and it was my day for the steamie and I couldnae get my sheets dried.' Andrew paused, and I heard him light up a fag and take a long deep draw. 'So what do you reckon, has he got cancer or no'?' he asked.

'Well, I've been trying to phone him for days to find

out and I was beginning to think he was already dead and buried when I got a text from him just yesterday,' I said.

'A text message?' Andrew said. 'Fuckssake, how did he manage to work out how to send one of them?'

'I don't know, I couldnae believe it myself. Anyway, the message just said he was fine and he left his mobile number so I gave him a bell this morning.'

'Right, so tell me, tell me – is it true? Does he have cancer?'

'Well, he didn't mention any cancer to me when I spoke with him this morning but what I can confirm is that he does have a bad case of constipation and now has extremely high blood pressure and the doctor thinks the two might be connected in some way. Mind you, since he saw the doctor he's made a few drastic lifestyle changes. Apparently he's stopped drinking and smoking, and he's eating fruit and vegetables every day and a serving of fresh fish once a week. Christ, next you know he'll be at the church on Sunday. That's all we fuckin' need.' I said.

'Christ Almighty. So what you're saying is he's not on his death bed?' Andrew asked, unable to conceal his disappointment.

'Well, I never heard of anybody die of constipation, Nobbie, but you never know. I'll keep you posted on that front. So, got any smart-arsed ideas for a wee story for me then? I'm desperate for inspiration. I can't seem to write a word at the minute.'

'Hey, I've got an idea. You could write a wee story called "Oh No, My Da's No' Got Cancer",' Andrew said.

'That's in bad taste, Nobbie, don't you think? Seriously, have you got any ideas for me?'

'Well, Blinky, if you're having a few issues with your creative outlet, answer this question. How are you feeling about life in general at the moment?'

'What do you want to know that for?' I asked

'Just answer the fuckin' question, will you?'

'I feel great right now.'

'Right, well there's your problem right there. You're not depressed enough to write. You take it from me, Blinky, the more depressed you are, the better your stories will be. The fuckin' ideas'll come flying out of your head without you having to think about them. What you need in your life is some kind of tragedy or drama or somethin' like that.'

'Christ, you know what, Nobbie, it's true – since I met Thomas I've been happier than I've ever been, so I probably could be doing with a bit more drama or some kind of tragedy in my life. I think you're right! Ah, now I can almost feel those waves of depression lapping up against the shore as we speak. Thanks, Nobbie, I really appreciate your input.'

'Don't worry about it, darlin'. You know you can always turn to your family in your time of need. That's what we're here for – to keep you depressed.'

'Aye, and what a great job you all do at it too.'

A bottle of Laphroaig

My da ended up selling the bungalows and his precious land and he moved away to the country with Mum. When I went back to Scotland from Sydney years later, I drove past the bungalows and I stopped to see how they had changed. I stared at the houses from the street and thought back to the days when I was Bruce's assistant and how I'd carried that hod full of bricks up that ladder all day long and I thought about the sandwiches we ate with our filthy hands and how we'd earned our tea and I remembered loving every minute of it.

I parked my car and I walked down the driveway towards the bungalows that now stood vacant and neglected and I walked across to Bruce's bungalow and I cupped my hands around my eyes and peered through the window and into his living room. I could still make out the lilac walls we'd laughed at and I imagined the two armchairs in front of the fire where we'd shared our spaghetti Bolognese and our glass of red wine with a spoonful of sugar in it and the memory of those times left me happy and sad at the same time.

Then I walked across to our bungalow and the concrete lions that Mum and I had bought that day at the Biggar auction still graced each side of the front doors. And when I walked around to our old back garden, I could almost see Nanny making her way to our back door wearing her beanie and Grampa's leather slippers and she's holding her bag of goodies high in the air to show me and she's smiling and I wish I could hold her and hug her and take away all the pain she suffered and I wish I could have offered her comfort and peace in the last few years of her life when she'd needed it most. All we'd wanted back then was harmony and the comfort that comes from living in close proximity to those you love and all of that was wasted by my da and his greed of gold.

After Mum left him, my da stayed on in the house they'd bought in the country. The house was a 100-year-old sandstone farmhouse called 'Glengarry', set high on a hill with views to Tinto Hill that, from a distance, looked remarkably like Mount Fuji. There were fireplaces in every room and an acre of land with crab-apple trees, overgrown bramble bushes and a solitary Victoria plum tree, heavy with fruit.

Mum had taken hardly anything that day she fled with her tartan holdall and the dogs and cats in the back of the car. But she'd come back from time to time to take all that was precious to her, like the photographs of Nanny and Grampa on holiday at the Palace of Versailles, of me and Izzy blowing out the candles on my first birthday cake, and of Andrew in his school uniform with his ears sticking out and smiling like a monkey.

After a long time living apart, Mum told my da she wanted a divorce and he didn't take it too bad, like an adult you might say. And so 'Glengarry' went up for sale, and my da made his own 'For Sale' sign and nailed it to a two-by-two post and stabbed it into the front lawn. He got enquiries all right, 'cause everybody who drove past wished they could live in this spot. 'Glengarry' overlooked the Mousebank River that twinkled like Irish eyes, and creamy-coloured lambs dotted grassy green fields as far as the eye could see. Even some famous racing-car driver enquired when he saw the garden at the back was big enough for a heli-pad to land his own personal helicopter. And every time Mum drove past a house for sale after that, Andrew would say, 'That's nae good tae us, Mum, where would we park our helicopter?' and all of us would laugh.

Hogmanay was approaching and that's the time for being with friends – and family, if you must; a time for tall dark handsome men with lumps of coal to come knocking on your door to first foot you; a time for black bun and steak-pie dinners and Tennent's Lager out of cans with pictures of dolly birds on the side, and the best malt whisky money can buy. Hogmanay's a time for cleaning your house from top to bottom too, 'cause your house must be clean for when the bells welcome in the New Year at midnight. In the village where 'Glengarry' stood they didn't listen out for the bells, but for the twelve rifle shots that rang out in the crisp midnight air.

Since Mum left, my da had spent his Hogmanays alone. One Hogmanay, Callum, the farmer from the farm across the road, invited my da to come just before midnight and have a dram with him and a few of the other farmers. Callum's wife, Moira, was putting on a spread – spicy aubergine dip, kalamata olives and curried cocktail sausages by all accounts. My da, he doesn't like all that foreign shite, but he'd go for the dram and the chat in any case.

At half past eleven my da put on the new Aran jumper he'd been keeping good for an occasion as special as this. Before he left he put his long-distance specs in his pocket and picked up his carry-out bag. He'd gone all out and bought a bottle of Laphroaig malt whisky to take with him, well, it was Hogmanay after all. At twenty-five minutes to midnight, he turned the kitchen light off, closed the door behind him, and started the walk to Callum's place, half a mile up the dirt track.

By the time he got to Callum's the drams were flowing freely and, my, was my da popular that night when he arrived with his bottle of Laphroaig. He put it on the table next to Moira's spicy aubergine dip and he wondered why nobody did cheese cubes and silverskin pickled onions on cocktail sticks stuck in an orange wrapped in silver paper like in the good old days, when a party was a party and you knew what the fuck you were eating.

After the first couple of drams, the electricity at Callum's place failed and the lights went out, and, sure, the electricity going off was a regular occurrence in the village in winter. And if it wasn't the electricity going off, it was the gas, and if it wasn't the gas, it was the water. Once when the water went off it wasn't the fault of the Water Board but my da who was digging holes in the garden with his digger and dug down too far and broke the main water pipe that supplied water to the entire village. Mum never saw him jump so fast from the cabin of his digger, screaming for her to phone the Water Board straightaway. The men from the Water Board came as soon as they could, mind it was six hours later, by which time enough water had gushed out of that pipe to service the whole of the African continent. It whooshed straight through Mum's petunias, uprooting them on its way down the sloping driveway and out onto the public road like Niagara fucking Falls. It was freezing cold that day and as the gushing slowed the water froze over until the road looked like a slow-moving glacier and the drivers approaching in their cars slammed on their brakes before they hit it and reversed back out and took the long way round to their destinations.

Moira the farmer's wife got a stack of candles out of the cupboard and everybody lit one and the party carried on. Big Bob was at the kitchen sink filling a jug of water for the whiskies and he peered through Moira's kitchen window across several fields to 'Glengarry' and he put on his glasses to take a second look. 'Looks like the power's back on in your place, Joe,' he said. My da stepped up to the window to see what Bob was going on about 'cause the power wasn't back on in Moira's. He took his long-distance specs out of his pocket and put them on only to discover he'd brought his telly specs. 'Ah, fuck it,' he said under his breath. He put them on anyway and screwed up his eyes and pressed his nose against Moira's kitchen window and, sure enough, he could see a flickering light. Only it seemed to be getting bigger. He took off his glasses, rubbed his eyes and looked again.

'Jesus Christ, the place is on fire!' he screamed, and he dropped his glass of Laphroaig and ran like hell back down the dirt track towards 'Glengarry' with three burly farmers in hot pursuit. By the time they were halfway there the entire front of the house was engulfed, but they kept on running and the freezing New Year's air scraped at the inside lining of their windpipes already raw from the Laphroaig and Moira's spicy dip.

By the time they got to the front gate it was too late. The fire had already taken hold and the searing orange flames roared much like my da used to roar as they ate their way through every room in the house. And the three burly farmers and my da looked helplessly on.

My da's cherry buns

'Good afternoon, ladies and gentlemen. This is your cabin crew supervisor speaking. Air Canada is pleased to announce the arrival of Flight 3245 from Alberta via Halifax. Welcome to Glasgow International Airport. We hope you have a pleasant stay. For your information, please note the following facts about Scotland; one, it rains, and two, it's cold.

'Please also note that all Scottish people are fully aware of these two facts. Consequently, after your stay here, please try to resist the temptation to tell every Scottish person you should meet hereafter that you went to Scotland once and, one, it rained, and two, it was cold.

'On behalf of the captain and crew, I would like to wish you a very safe and enjoyable stay. Thank you for choosing Air Canada.'

Uncle Jack had gone back to Scotland for a wedding and he decided he'd drop in on my da when he arrived, so he took a taxi from the airport and went straight to my da's new house. Later, when my da phoned me in Sydney, he told me he couldn't believe his eyes when he opened the door and saw Jack standing there. Not because he hadn't seen his brother for ten years, but more the shock of seeing somebody actually wearing one of those ridiculous ten-gallon hats like the one John Wayne wore in *How the West was Won*.

'Well, are ya not gonna say anything? Are ya not pleased to see me?' Jack asked with this stupid Yankee twang he must've picked up on his ranch, '*hangin' aboot wi' his Yankee pals*', my da said. My da never made any distinction between the Yanks and the Canadians. All spoke funny and wore fucking ridiculous ten-gallon hats.

And my da's opening statement was what you might expect from him, having not set eyes on his brother for ten years. 'There's nae spare bed here,' he said, 'you'll have to go somewhere else.' Warmth and compassion are not my da's strong points. Mind you, I couldn't tell you what his strong points were, except of course maybe his ability to park any vehicle you care to mention – and to perfection – but that's for another time. My da stood at the door and stared at Jack and said nothing.

'Aren't ya gonna invite me in?' Jack asked.

'Aye, awright, but I'm just on my way oot. I've a pick-up to make at Auchterarder, then I'm dropping the same load off at Auchtermuchty, so I'll need to be making tracks.

You'll need to get goin' as well, will you no'? I mean, you'll need to find somewhere to sleep tonight before the night starts to draw in, eh?'

'Can I at least have a cuppa tea before I head off?'

'Aye, awright,' my da said, 'but you'll need to make it quick.' And my da switched on his new fast-boiling cordless electric kettle he got only the week before from Lewis's department store on Argyle Street with the six million Fly Buy points he'd accrued. This new kettle would have the water boiled up in an instant and he'd be rid of Jack in no time. Jack looked around the house while the kettle boiled.

'It's really small, isn't it?'

'What's small?'

'Your place here.'

'It's big enough for me! Since "Glengarry" burnt doon, this is all I need. Plus I'm a single man now and thank fuck for that. It's been a few years since Betty left me and to be honest, I've never looked back. Now I've only masel' to think about and I do what I like wi' my wages at the end of the week. I've even enough money to buy masel' a fancy car these days and so long as I've got my *Sale of the Century* and *Come On Down!* for company at night, there's nothin' more I need.'

'Back in Canada, our ranch house has ten bedrooms and four bathrooms,' Jack said. 'We just like a bit of space, you know, for when our friends drop by. We're pretty isolated out there – it's a nine-hour drive from the nearest village and when the snow comes in winter, we sometimes can't get off the property for weeks on end. It's pretty extreme living, but we love it that way. We just love the space, the isolation, you know, just working the land, being at one with the cows that we breed. Just being there with nature, you know?'

'No, I don't fuckin' know. What do you want to live away oot there for – in the middle of nowhere? Are you fuckin' mad or what?'

'No, Joe. It's just a choice that Georgina and I made and we're glad we did. We've got everything we could ever want out there and we've got over a million dollars in the bank. Life's good, you know?'

'If you've got a million dollars in the bank, how come you're wearing that stupid fuckin' hat then?'

'What d'ya mean? These hats are all the rage in downtown Alberta. You wear a hat like this out there and it says something about the kind of man you are.'

'Aye, and you wear a hat like that in this town and it says something about the kind of man you are too – that you're a fuckin' dick. So take it off and don't embarrass me. I've my reputation to think of.'

And so my da made the tea and put extra milk in Jack's so it would be cool enough for him to drink down quickly and knocked back his own mug of tea, slamming it down on the kitchen table to let Jack know that the tea break was at an end. And Jack just sat there.

'Well, I've got to be off,' my da said. 'Got to get down the yard and get the lorry ready for action. Just pull the door shut on your way out. Cheerio.'

'So long, partner, I'll catch you before I head back to Alberta.'

'Och, don't worry about that, I'm sure you've plenty to be doin' without coming back here to see me. I'll be fine. See you in another ten years. Cheerio.'

And with that, my da jumped into his Rover 3000 and drove around the corner to the yard to get his lorry ready for the next job. Twenty minutes later, my da was in the yard when he heard this Yankee accent and turned around to see Jack strut into the yard, wearing that fucking hat, the checked shirt and, Christ Almighty, cowboy boots. And as if that wasn't bad enough, he stopped to talk to the lads in the yard and my da hunched himself up and tried to hide under the bonnet of his lorry . Next, the lads were shouting across the yard at the top of their voices, 'Hey, Joe, here's your brother lookin' fur ye! Ye didnae tell us you had a brother fae Americy.'

'It's Canada, actually,' Jack corrected.

'Canada, Americy, it's aw' the same to us, pal,' the lads said.

My da looked up from under the bonnet and wished he was somewhere else, and Jack strutted up and stopped at the lorry and looked under the bonnet at my da. My da stopped what he was doing and looked up at Jack from the engine.

'Did you want somethin'?' he asked Jack.

'Yeah. You don't have any butter in your fridge.'

My da stood up straight at that point with his greasy spanner and oily rag in his hand and looked at Jack square in the eyes. 'Did you come all this way just to tell me that?'

'Well, yeah, I did.'

'I suppose you noticed I don't have any bread in my bread bin either?'

'Yeah, that too. I'm going to the baker's to pick up something to eat, so how about giving me your house key so I can get back in to finish my tea?' Jack said.

'Aye, awright, here's the key,' my da said, thrusting the key into Jack's hands. 'And look, I'll come back home masel' shortly and change into my boiler suit before I head off and I'll have a bite wi' you since you're going to the baker's. Now, don't go into Gregory's the baker, by the way, their stuff's helluva greasy. Go tae Smith's and ask for big Janice. Tell her you're my brother and you'll get a fresh-cream strawberry tart thrown in. Actually, naw, on second thoughts, don't tell *anybody* you're my brother. Just get what you want and I'll see you back at the house. And don't forget, you'll need to get goin' soon – you've still a bed to find fur the night.'

Jack swaggered out of the yard in his ten-gallon hat, and my da pretended to be engrossed in what was under the bonnet and he didn't dare look at the lads in the yard.

He'd never been so embarrassed in his life except maybe for that time he was drunk and got out of his bed during the night, opened the middle drawer in the chest of drawers next to his bed, pissed into it, closed the drawer and went back to bed. And when he got out of bed in the morning he stood in his own piss and started screaming at the dogs for pissing in the bedroom during the night and that's when Mum said the dogs were smart, but she'd never heard of a dog opening a drawer to piss in it.

Back at the yard my da did his final oil and water checks and closed the bonnet tight, wiped his oily hands down the sides of his trousers and hopped back into his Rover 3000 and headed home for his quick bite.

Jack had managed to find the baker and big Janice must've been on duty, 'cause there was the tell-tale fresh-cream strawberry tart sitting on the table, and right beside the tart were three cherry buns topped with white icing and half a maraschino cherry. My da pulled up a chair, anxious to join in the feast, and as he leaned forward to grab a cherry bun he noticed his hands were still thick with oil and grease so he ducked outside to the wash house to give his hands a good scrub with that Grease Away stuff that lorry drivers and hard men use.

'You wouldnae believe it,' he told me on the phone. 'I comes back fae scrubbing my oily hands and there's Jack, polishing off the last scrap of patisserie on the table – *including big Janice's fresh-cream strawberry tart* – which by law was rightfully mine. Can you believe that? The greedy bastard ate every last crumb himself and left nothing for me. It's hard to think a man could treat his ain brother like that – I mean, after ten years of not seeing each other, the least you'd think he could do would be to share his cherry buns wi' his own brother, do you no' think?'

'Well,' I said to my da, 'if a man cannae share his cherry buns with his own brother, it's a bad day. I mean, Christ Almighty, is it any wonder he's got a million dollars in the bank if that's how he carries on?'

'Exactly, hen,' my da said, 'it's a sad day when a man treats his own flesh and blood like that. I mean, my own brother – *ten years* we havnae seen each other and this is what it's come to. Incidentally, did you see that heavy fall of snow last night? I wonder if he managed to find a bed for the night before the blizzard came on. I hope he got caught in it, the uncharitable bastard.'

Brief conversations with
my da

We don't speak much, me and my da. He still lives by himself in Scotland and what with me on the other side of the world in Sydney, we only speak maybe twice a year, which suits us both fine.

And I forgive him now, sort of, and mostly my heart breaks for him when I think of him so lonely. Mum, though, she continues to be the loving mother she's always been, seeing nothing but good in me, Izzy and Andrew and everything we do. But she's hard on herself for having stayed as long as she did with my da and for what she sees as wasting her life and there's nothing any of us can say that will ever change her mind.

Mind you, since Mum left him, my da's worked seven days a week running his own portaloo transportation business. And the hand-written sign on the door of his articulated lorry reads 'Big Joe's Transport – Portaloos moved *night and day*' and he does the work himself, dropping a hundred toilets a day on building sites all the way from Glasgow to John O'Groats and back again. And so it's no wonder he's got more money in the bank now than he knows what to do with and he doesn't have to think twice about buying himself fancy new cars whenever the notion comes upon him. So when we do speak, it tends to be about my car or his car, my work or his work or something really annoying that somebody has done to him recently. He rang me the other day and our conversation went much the same as the last time he rang me.

'So, how's your wee car runnin'?' he asked.

'Funny you should ask, but I just traded it in this week for a brand new one, da. The old one was just getting to that stage where it needed new brake shoes and maybe even a new carburettor, whatever that is, so I just got rid of it.'

'Aye, that's for the best I think – trade it in and get a new one, then you don't have the heartache when it doesn't run properly,' he said.

'Especially when I don't have anybody I can call on here in Sydney to replace the brake pads for me when I need it. Don't get me wrong, da, you were a useless father, but at least you could replace a brake pad on my car,' I said, paying him the biggest compliment I ever had.

'Whit dae ye mean, useless faithir? That's a bit rough, is it no'?' he said.

'Rough or no' da, it's the truth. Like it or lump it. So, how's *your* car runnin' anyway?'

'Like a sweetie – absolutely beautiful.'

'And what are you drivin' these days?'

And so he went on to tell me about how he was driving past the showroom on Merrylees Road the week before in his lorry full of portaloos and he saw the silver Jaguar of his dreams in the window and that he fell in love with it straightaway. So he parked the lorry at the front of the showroom window and went inside wearing his boiler suit and wiping his hands on the rag he keeps in his pocket for wiping his greasy hands on. And the salesman didn't get up from his desk and hardly even looked in my da's direction. My da asked him was he not going to serve him, and the salesman looked him up and down in his boiler suit with the greasy hands and he asked my da what he wanted. My da pointed to the silver Jaguar in the window and said, 'I want that.' And the salesman looked my da up and down again and asked him if he thought he could afford it and my da said, 'I've mair money in my bank account than you'll ever have in this fuckin' lifetime, ya wee prick!' So the salesman told my da how much it was and my da put his greasy rag down on the salesman's desk and took his chequebook out and paid for the car there and then, and the salesman started kissing my da's arse.

'And so I got it delivered yesterday,' he said. 'And wait

till I tell you this, you'll never believe it. I drove it up to Lanark this morning for a haircut and an ice cream.'

'You're far travelled for a haircut and an ice cream are you no'?' I said.

'I suppose I am,' he said, 'but she's a lovely wee lassie that cuts it and she charges me the pensioner rate so I usually get myself an ice cream with the change from one of those newfangled gella-toria bars or whatever the fuck they're called these days.'

'Aye, it's a gelateria. So what flavour do you get anyway?' I asked him.

'I like the straight vanilla,' he said. 'But sometimes I get the Lanark Hokey Cokey.'

'Oh, that sounds nice. Has it got crunchy bits in it?'

'Aye, it does, mind you the crunchy bits get under my plate and I have to rinse my teeth under the tap at the kitchen sink when I get home.'

'Anyway, so what happened when you went to Lanark?'

'Well, I parked in my usual spot, just in behind the Crown Hotel there, you know, on the corner just after Wee Tommy's Pie Shop and while I remember to tell you, the pie shop's just been bought out by Pies R Us, if you can believe that. So I'm coming out of the gellatoria wi' my cone and the Lanark Hokey Cokey's bloody meltin' and runnin' down my fingers, I hate it when my fingers get all sticky like that, and I'm lickin' the fuckin' ice cream to stop it running any further down the cone, when I looks up and you wouldnae believe what I saw with my own eyes.'

'Naw, whit did you see, da?'

'Some bastard has only come out of the nursery, bought themselves a tray of bedding plants for their herbaceous fuckin' border, and left the tray on the bonnet of my fuckin' silver Jaguar! *My fuckin' silver Jaguar!* Can you fuckin' believe that? Right there, on the bonnet of my fuckin' silver Jaguar? I don't know about you, but I just couldnae fuckin' believe that.'

'That's fuckin' unbelievable, da. So what did you do?'

'Well, I grabbed the tray of bedding plants, threw them on the ground and stood on every last one of them. Then I got into the car and finished my cone and went into the glove box and brought out a packet of those things your mother used to buy, what are they called, Wet Things, or something like that.'

'Wet Ones.'

'Wet Things, Wet Ones, whatever. And so I wiped my fingers on one of them, threw the wrapper of the cone and the Wet One oot the windae and headed for home.'

'Right, I see,' I said. And then there was silence.

'So how's it going for you at work?' he asked.

'Fine,' I said. 'How's it going for you at work?'

'Fine,' he said. And there was another silence.

'Well, I better be goin' then, Ali. It was nice talkin' to you, hen. Maybe talk to you again in six months, eh?'

'Aye, awright, da, if you've a mind.'

'Awright, Ali. Cheerio then, hen,' he said.

'Cheerio, da.'

Alison Whitelock

Born and bred in Scotland, Alison left behind the mountains and rivers and ballads of bonnie Morag when she was thirty years old. A fan of Patsy Cline and the occasional pineapple tart with a cup of PG Tips, she lives with her endlessly patient chain-smoking French husband Thomas in a trendy suburb of Sydney they simply can't afford. While she enjoys brown rice, tofu and organic produce, she continues to shave her legs and refuses to wear Birkenstocks, especially with black ankle socks and khaki shorts. She has no children to speak of unless you count her cats Angus and Nellie. *Poking Seaweed with a stick and running away from the smell* is her first book. Her da hopes it will be her last.

Thanks

To my darling husband Thomas whose encouragement, love and patience seem to know no bounds.

To Alison and Hugh at Polygon for believing in the book and liking what they read.

To Julia, Angela, Michael and Stephanie at Wakefield Press in South Australia for everything so far.